Everything Isn't Terrible

Conquer Your Insecurities, Interrupt Your Anxiety, and Finally Calm Down

Dr. Kathleen Smith

BOOKS

New York Boston

Copyright © 2019 by Annie Kathleen Smith
Cover design by Raina Tinker
Cover copyright © 2019 Hachette Book Group, Inc.

Hachette Books
Hachette Book Group
1290 Avenue of the Americas, New York, NY 10104
HachetteBooks.com
Twitter.com/HachetteBooks
Instagram.com/HachetteBooks

Printed in the United States of America

First Edition: December 2019

Published by Hachette Books, an imprint of Perseus Books, LLC, a subsidiary of Hachette Book Group, Inc. The Hachette Books name and logo is a trademark of the Hachette Book Group.

The publisher is not responsible for websites (or their content) that are not owned by the publisher.

Library of Congress Cataloging-in-Publication Data has been applied for.

ISBNs: 978-0-31649-2539 (hardcover), 978-0-31649-2553 (ebook)

LSC-C

10 9 8 7 6 5 4 3 2 1

for Jacob, my partner in differentiation

Contents

CONTENTS

Part Four
Your Anxious World

Introduction

We truly live in anxious times. In a recent public opinion poll, the American Psychiatric Association reported that a majority of Americans are anxious about their safety, their health, their finances, their relationships, and, of course, politics. We fight on Facebook, we flee the Thanksgiving table, or we freeze up and hope someone calmer will solve the world's problems. Stuck on high alert, we've stopped looking at the facts and started assessing situations based on our feelings. We're reacting instead of acting, leading, and calming the hell down.

I live and work as a therapist in perhaps the most anxious city in America: Washington, DC. Many of my clients want to be beacons of calmness and wisdom in our anxious world. Others just want to get through the day without snapping at their mother or stalking their ex's Instagram. They rely heavily on encouragement from others. Some of them fear vulnerability in their relationships or avoid their anxious coworkers. Others simply feel overwhelmed by the dumpster fire that is our country right now. Sound familiar?

At the end of the day, we all just want long-term, life-altering change. We all want to live a life guided by principle rather than fear or worry. And deep down, we do have the capacity to calm ourselves. We are capable of shutting off our autopilot and grabbing the controls. And by choosing how we handle our anxiety, we choose our fate. So let me tell you about a theory that changed my life.

What's Bowen Theory?

Every therapist has a theory that guides them in their work with clients. Mine is a theory of human behavior known as Bowen theory. Murray Bowen was a psychiatrist and the father of family psychotherapy. He was from Tennessee, just like me, and I liked his brilliant yet folksy way of describing relationships. Traditional therapists focused on individual people, but Dr. Bowen believed that we could only learn to calm down when we looked at our relationship systems. Because when we feel anxious, we often try to make other people change. We try to calm everyone else down so we can finally relax. But if you can work on managing yourself in these relationships, it's likely that your family, your workplace, and even the greater world will calm down a little too.

Dr. Bowen taught that if anxiety is generated in our relationships, then it can also be fixed in relationships. Therefore, long-term change doesn't happen in isolation, or even on a therapist's couch. It happens when we're willing to work on being our best selves in our most difficult relationships. I realize this sounds gross and hard, but boy, does it make a difference. If a person can learn to think and act for herself in her anxious family, her anxious community, and her anxious world, then her sense of self won't be so dependent on the cooperation of others.

I'd love for you to think that I'm a genius, but many of the ideas in the book come straight from Bowen theory. You don't need to be an expert in theory to read this book. But if you're interested in learning more, I've included some basic definitions and resources at the back to help you get started.

Okay, But How Do I Calm Down?

Each chapter in this book will examine a particular arena of life where anxiety can get you into trouble. We'll take a look at your anxious self, your relationships, your career, and the broader world.

I'll use examples from my therapy work to help you get a better picture of what it looks like to build a stronger self and reduce overall anxiety. To protect the confidentiality of my clients, names and identifying information have been changed. Each example is a composite of many people with similar challenges. You may find that you see yourself in a number of these people. I certainly do.

Building a solid, principled self is a complex and lifelong process. To keep you from feeling too overwhelmed, I'll rely on three verbs throughout the book: **observing**, **evaluating**, and **interrupting** your anxious functioning.

First, you have to start observing. Before you can change your anxious behaviors, you need to know what they are. By observing yourself, you're already using the part of your brain that helps calm you down. Much of the book will illustrate the common behaviors that accompany anxiety, so you can become an expert at recognizing them.

Second, you have to evaluate your behavior. You have to take a hard look at what you do to manage your anxiety, and ask yourself, "Is this who I really want to be?" I'll talk about how to live a life that is guided by thinking and by principle, and not by freaking the hell out.

Third, you have to interrupt what's automatic. Once you've observed your automatic behaviors, and decided how you really want to live, you have to start looking for opportunities to interrupt your autopilot. This implies a certain level of discomfort. Because any time you do something you wouldn't normally do, it's a little uncomfortable. Or a lot.

After working on building a more solid self, people often comment that their previous life is totally unrecognizable from their current one. They spend less energy seeking approval and have more energy to work on their goals. They have fewer emotional and physical symptoms. Their relationships are more vulnerable and less anxious.

Some may argue that focusing on yourself while our world is on fire is selfish. But I think the real problem is that there's not enough "self" in how we respond to the challenges we face. The calmest people will emerge as the change makers, because they understand that in the anxious equation of today's world, you are the only variable you can manipulate.

By changing yourself, you change the equation. By building a more solid self, you might help calm down your family, your community, and the entire planet. That's pretty damn powerful.

Part One

✳ ✳ ✳

YOUR ANXIOUS SELF

CHAPTER 1

Focusing on Yourself

All his life has he looked away, to the future, to the horizon. Never his mind on where he was, hmm? What he was doing.

—*Yoda*, The Empire Strikes Back

Jordan spent most of her first appointment telling me about Kyle, her ex-boyfriend. Kyle had a history of freaking out when things got serious. He feared intimacy because he didn't have a stable relationship with his parents. He had used Jordan to find a job and fight his depression, and then promptly dropped her. Jordan and Kyle were no longer a couple, but they still hung out in the same friend group and occasionally had sex. She told me that she followed Kyle on Venmo to see what "dumb" things he was buying for other women. She knew his email password and logged in to see his dating app notifications. Jordan had blocked Kyle on Instagram during a moment of rage, but her friends texted her the pictures he posted while partying with twenty-two-year-olds. "Honestly, I'm embarrassed for him," she said.

You might want to laugh, but I'm not going to throw the first stone here. We have all been Jordan in one way or another. To be human is to be focused on another human, especially when it's a romantic relationship. While Jordan gave me her dissertation on Kyle, I realized

I knew nothing about this woman that didn't relate to her ex. Her mind was completely fixed on Kyle, and I could feel the anxiety radiating off of her.

This is the first and most daunting challenge for any therapist: to help a person begin to focus on herself. It's ironic, considering that many people label therapy as a selfish practice. The reality is that there's rarely enough *self* in it. So many people come through the door ready to complain about their partner, their parents, or their boss. They know that they're anxious, but they don't see how focusing their attention outward, what I call "other-focus," contributes to their anxiety. Therefore, the first step in calming down is simply to begin to think about yourself. To see how your anxiety is at work. It sounds easy, but it isn't.

What Is Anxiety?

It's not surprising that Jordan was uber-focused on Kyle. The habit of focusing on others has biological origins. When we feel threatened, we must respond to the threat. This is the simplest and best definition of anxiety: anxiety is your response to a real or imagined threat.

Our anxiety serves a very important purpose, because the central goal of being a human is simple: to not die for as long as you can. One might call this, oh I don't know... *living*. But in your quest to live, there are a lot of things in the world that threaten you. Bears. Earthquakes. Chipotle. Kyle. Fortunately, evolution has given humans a way of surviving scary things.

You can:
(a) **fight** scary thing
(b) **flee** from scary thing
(c) **freeze** to hide from scary thing
(d) **fret** to others about scary thing

Most organisms have some or all of these built-in responses to danger, but we humans are special. Not only can we sense danger, but we can *imagine* potential danger. Your dog doesn't worry about whether you'll feed him tomorrow. He only wants to know if you're going to finish that piece of cheese. Our ability to perceive danger has helped us survive and thrive. But like any superpower, it can cause problems. We end up worrying too much about hypothetical threats and not the reality-based problems of today.

Because humans have different genes, families, and experiences, we vary in how sensitive we are to imagined threats. Think of it as a built-in alarm system. Some of us have alarms that trigger very easily, and others do not. Maybe your alarm only goes off when there's a real fire, but mine will sound when I've only slightly burned the chicken nuggets.

Our alarms also can evolve based on our encounters with real threats. You're going to be more anxious after you've seen a bear than on a regular Tuesday with no bears. (In case you can't tell, I'm very concerned about bears.) When your alarm sounds, you don't exactly have time to self-reflect. If you stop to self-reflect when you're being chased by a bear, then you're toast. You know that the bear is the cause of your distress, so you need to escape it as quickly as possible. Most human relationships, however, are more complex. But the more we feel threatened, the more we apply the same cause-and-effect thinking to our relationships. Our brain shifts to the tunnel vision that plagued Jordan. We want one person to be the bear, so we make them one. To protect ourselves, we invest a great deal of energy into becoming experts on someone we can't control, that is, the Kyles of the world.

Much of the world today is caught in a state of other-focus. We feel frightened by many things, so we see many bears. Republicans. Democrats. Family members. People who don't agree with us. People who don't look like us. No wonder everything feels terrible.

The Trouble with "Why"

When someone tells you to focus on yourself, it can feel like the other person is getting off the hook. You might think, "Aren't some people just terrible? Doesn't Kyle play a role in the dysfunction of this relationship?" You bet he does, simply by being a human. But when Jordan became anxious about the state of their relationship, she could only see Kyle's part. Jordan knew that Kyle's behaviors were a part of the problem, so she labeled him as the *cause* of the problem. She saw Kyle as the person who must change to free her from her anxious email snooping. By focusing on Kyle, she had given up her own agency.

There are many ways we get caught in the trap of focusing on others. When we really want someone to like us, or we worry about someone we love, we lose sight of ourselves. When someone disagrees with us or hurts us, we try to calm down by changing or blaming the other person.

Focusing on another person can also look like:
- giving them excessive advice
- trying to motivate them
- worrying about them
- complaining about them
- stalking them on social media
- guessing what they're thinking
- going out of your way to avoid them
- doing things for them they can do themselves

Humans end up in this cause-and-effect thinking because we're programmed to ask the question "Why?" when we're anxious. Asking why implies fault. It conveniently gives us someone or something to blame. Jordan was asking herself, "Why am I so unhappy?" And she had an obvious answer to this question: "Because Kyle is a tool." The problem was that Kyle was not sitting in therapy. Jordan was there, and Jordan was the only variable she could alter in this grand equation of dysfunction. To help her focus on herself, I simply asked Jordan a bunch of questions that didn't start with "why."

Me: When does Kyle make you anxious?
Jordan: When he doesn't return my texts.

Me: What do you do when he doesn't return them?
Jordan: I blow up his phone or call a friend to check his Instagram.

Me: How effective has that been?
Jordan: It feels good in the moment to attack him. But then I feel terrible when I don't get what I want. I feel more anxious.

Me: What could be more effective at calming you down? What ideas do you have?
Jordan: I could probably not check my phone as much. Or maybe try and take some deep breaths instead.

Weeks passed, and I tried to keep Jordan focused on how she wanted to respond to this situation with Kyle. There were glimmers of self-focus, but her attention always shifted back to her ex. She tried to teach Kyle how to not talk about other women when they were together. She tried to convince Kyle that they needed couples counseling to work on their relationship. She hypothesized why Kyle was too immature and would never change. Jordan put so much of her energy into trying to manage Kyle's emotions, thoughts, and behaviors. The only thing that calmed her down after a fight was getting an apology text from him. No wonder she was so tired and so anxious. She had forgotten that someone else besides Kyle could calm her down—herself!

Over time, Jordan's focus began to shift back to herself. Jordan started to notice how her relationships were a two-way street and that her own stress level affected her functioning and level of maturity. She observed how she arrived late to work when her boss was in a bad mood. She saw that she was more likely to fight with her mother on the phone when she had been drinking. By noticing the part she played in every important relationship, she was ready to take responsibility for her functioning. Because that's what responsibility is—the ability to respond. Jordan could see that if she learned to focus on being her best self in her relationships, a lot of the drama would simply fizzle out.

How quickly a person can get to this place of self-focus depends on a few things. One variable is how strong their sense of self is. We'll talk more about this concept in the following chapters, but the idea is that we all have varying levels of how other-focused we tend to be. A second variable is how much stress is present. Maybe you can stay self-focused during a mildly challenging event. But if the stress keeps getting cranked up, it can become difficult even for the most mature person to not shift into blame-focused thinking that asks, "Why?"

Let's Practice!

One way of strengthening your ability to focus on yourself is to practice flipping other-focused questions into self-focused ones. Think of it as hitting the reverse camera button on your phone in order to take a selfie. Here are a few examples:

Other-focused: Why am I so anxious?
Self-focused: How do I manage my anxiety, and how effective is it?

Other-focused: Why doesn't my family understand me?
Self-focused: What part do I play in the immature functioning of my family?

Other-focused: Why do people pile too much on my plate?

Self-focused: What do I do for others that they can do for themselves?

Other-focused: Is my spouse really right for me?

Self-focused: How can I be the person I want to be in my marriage?

Other-focused: Why is America such a dumpster fire?

Self-focused: What is my responsibility as a citizen in this dumpster fire?

When you begin to focus on your part in a relationship or a problem, a funny thing will happen—you'll start to calm down! This is because you'll be focused on the one thing you can control: yourself.

My office became a place where Jordan could calm down a little bit and begin to think more about her anxious functioning. Over time, she got a good sense of how her intense focus on Kyle reinforced his desire to stay away from her. They were caught in the classic relationship dance of anxious pursuit and anxious flight. Jordan took the focus off Kyle and started working on her friendships, her health, and her career goals. She began to see that her happiness maybe *wasn't* dependent on Kyle's behavior. In other words, she calmed down. And can you guess what happened? Yep. They got back together. But now Jordan saw that her new challenge was to continue to take responsibility for herself and her anxiety while in a relationship with Kyle.

I don't know what happened to those two. People will often stop coming to therapy when things have calmed down. But I hope that Jordan found a way to keep thinking about herself when she was tempted to focus on Kyle. People can grow up and calm down within relationships or without them. But I'm still rooting for Jordan, because I know what it's like to get a small taste of your own capacity in life. I hope that she has continued to see how staying focused on herself will make her relationships a little less anxious.

Your Questions

Observe

- In what relationships do I tend to be focused on blaming others?
- When do I try to change others in order to manage my own anxiety?
- What emotions and physical symptoms do I experience when I'm other-focused?

Evaluate

- How does my focus on others conflict with the person I want to be?
- What might my best self be doing in situations in which I have tended to blame others?
- Is there any wisdom I'd like to remember in these situations?

Interrupt

- What are upcoming opportunities for me to practice being self-focused?
- How can I refrain from focusing on others as a way of managing my anxiety?
- What people and resources could help me be more self-focused?

Your Practice

Over the next twenty-four hours, make a note every time you find yourself focusing anxiously on another person. Examples could be when your significant other loads the dishwasher the wrong way or when someone says something on social media that infuriates you. You are other-focused anytime you want to manage the thoughts, emotions, or behaviors of another person, even if it's a stranger or a celebrity. At the end of the day, give yourself one kind pat on the back for every name on the list, and don't beat yourself up for how long it is. Paying attention is the most important part of change! The more you pay attention, the more likely you are to remember to stay focused on yourself.

CHAPTER 2

Thinking and Feeling

> Facts are stubborn things; and whatever may be our wishes, our inclinations, or the dictates of our passions, they cannot alter the state of facts and evidence.
>
> —John Adams

Monica's last therapist had abandoned her. At least, that's what it felt like to Monica. In reality, she had moved. But that's the thing about feelings. They're allergic to facts. When Monica came to meet with me, she quickly learned that I was more interested in hearing about the facts than her feelings. Because the facts of Monica's family were quite interesting. When Monica was in college, her father developed a gambling addiction. Fed up with his addiction, her mother went looking for support and ended up having multiple affairs. When the affairs came to light, her family exploded apart in an emotional shockwave. Monica's brother took her mother's side, and she took her father's.

Cut off from the rest of his family, Monica's father clung to her for emotional support. He accused her of betrayal if she talked to anyone on her mother's side of the family. He refused to address his gambling problem, and his debt grew by the hour. Things were pretty intense, because there wasn't a lot of emotional separation in Monica's family. They may have stopped talking to each other, but if you can't bear to be in the same room with someone, then you're not exactly emotionally separate from them.

Dr. Bowen proposed the idea that people will vary in the amount of emotional separation they have from their families. He had a word for this separation: differentiation. People who were more differentiated could be in close contact with an anxious group of people and retain their ability to think and act for themselves. No one can do this perfectly, but some people are more differentiated than others. People with low levels of differentiation struggle to separate their thoughts and emotions. They also have trouble telling the difference between their thoughts and feelings and someone else's thoughts and feelings.

No one in Monica's family could think like an individual. No one could treat anyone else like an individual. They related to each other based on what side they took in the divorce, and everyone had someone else to blame for their unhappiness. Monica struggled to think about her family history objectively. She was so connected to her father's thoughts and feelings about her mother's infidelity that she had adopted them as her own. If her father didn't like someone, then she assumed that they were toxic. Her mother became the main villain in the story of her family. She was the answer to that dangerous question, "Why?"

Differentiation Is the Goal

This ability to distinguish your thoughts and feelings from other people's thoughts and feelings is essential to calming down and getting stuff done. Think about it—if you called 911 and the operator also panicked, then they're not going to be very helpful. If people accepted everyone else's thinking, then we'd still assume you could sail right off the edge of the Earth. People's ability to think for themselves has literally changed the world.

Differentiation is the ability to:
1. separate thoughts from feelings
2. separate your thoughts and feelings from other people's

Monica had trouble distinguishing between thinking and feeling, between reality and the tunnel vision of anxiety. She thought she had escaped her family by cutting off contact, but her lack of emotional separation from her family was mirrored in how she operated with her coworkers and friends. When she sensed someone was upset, her emotions would spill over into her thinking. This made it difficult for Monica to stay in contact with reality and the facts. If her boss was upset, then it was her fault. If a friend was distraught, then they were definitely going to end their friendship with her. The stakes felt super high, even in benign situations.

The only way Monica knew to avoid anxiety was to make sure everyone around her was happy. Monica dedicated an enormous amount of energy into making sure her friends and coworkers liked her. She would listen to her father for hours on the phone. She answered emails at two a.m. to please her boss. She would always go over to her boyfriend's place so he didn't have to travel across town. She became an expert at reading facial expressions and voice tone to detect unhappiness in others. When her inner alarm went off, she put all her energy into pleasing or escaping. Monica had no energy left to take care of herself or work on her goals.

If a person can differentiate between their own thoughts and emotions, then everyone else's anxiety is a little less contagious. Differentiated people can be self-directed but also participate in intimate relationships, even when things are tense.

So how do you work on your level of differentiation? The answer is by focusing on yourself. To learn the difference between your thinking and feeling, you'll have to get to know your feelings a little bit better, because those jokers are not going anywhere.

Making Anxiety Your Friend

Our society treats anxiety like it's a tumor. We want to cut it out, starve it, or shrink it into oblivion. In therapy, people want to rate their progress by their level of anxiety. I watch people beat themselves up because they got anxious after a breakup, after a death, or when their flight gets canceled six times in a row. But in today's world, we know how much stressful events are out of our control. Your anxiety is a fellow passenger in the journey of life, so you might as well get to know this annoying sidekick.

I like to think of my anxiety as a smoke alarm. It's annoying but also important. A smoke alarm is designed to protect me from danger, but sometimes it will go off when I'm cooking and there's no real danger. When the alarm beeps, I do not run screaming out of the house. I don't beat it to death with a broom. I simply look around and see whether there's a fire. If there isn't one, then I reset the alarm. I understand that my smoke alarm is designed to be sensitive to protect me. It is my friend, and it might save my life one day.

Our alarm systems will vary in sensitivity based on our experiences in relationships, especially those within our families. Many of us have a sensitive alarm system installed in our brains. This has a lot to do with our level of differentiation. Sometimes your anxiety will yell, "*Fire!*" when there isn't a fire. It will shout, "*Danger!*" when you get a passive-aggressive text. But unlike the alarm in your kitchen, it can be difficult to remember that your anxiety is a sensitive system. Over time, the more you perceive imaginary threats, the more chronic anxiety you will have. Every time Monica got an email from her boss scheduling a meeting, her alarm was triggered. Objectively, she knew her job wasn't on the line, but emotionally, all hands were on deck. She would beat herself up for perceiving small events as big threats, for acting like the house was burning down. But shaming herself kept her stuck on high alert. We talked about how

15

staying curious could help her work on differentiation and reduce this chronic anxiety.

Being more differentiated, however, doesn't mean you turn into a robot. People who have a higher level of differentiation still feel anxiety. They're just able to override it by slowing down its escalation. They're better able to tell what's a real threat and what's an imaginary one, and they can switch off the autopilot and grab the controls. More differentiated people are also more skeptical when it comes to their emotions. Often our anxiety is like a sketchy news editor who wants to get the quickest scoop and the most clicks. It takes what's happening to you in the moment and creates terrifying click-bait headlines.

Experience: You get stood up on a date.
Anxiety headline: YOU WILL DIE ALONE WITH TEN CATS!

Experience: Your boss sends you a confusing email.
Anxiety headline: HOW TO SURVIVE ON THE STREETS WHEN YOU'RE FIRED TOMORROW

Experience: You hear a strange noise in your apartment.
Anxiety headline: ARE YOU STRONG ENOUGH TO DEFEND YOURSELF WITH THIS CURLING IRON?

Experience: You send a text to a new friend.
Anxiety headline: CONGRATULATIONS ON BEING *TIME MAGAZINE'S* MOST ANNOYING PERSON OF THE YEAR!

You can see how these headlines are attention-grabbing but not exactly reality-based. Your anxiety is like a Fox News correspondent.

Your thinking brain, however, is the calm NPR reporter who maybe hasn't found an exciting spin but is reporting the facts. So when you want to calm down, ask yourself, "What's the real story here?" And then let your inner Nina Totenberg tell you what's happening.

Here are some other common lies anxiety will tell people:
- This plane is definitely crashing.
- This person finds you extremely bothersome.
- Everyone you see on social media is better than you.
- You are definitely getting fired.
- No one understands you.
- There is a murderer behind the shower curtain!
- No one will ever hire you.
- You are unlovable.

Anxiety uses words like *never, no one, definitely, enough, should,* and *always.* It encourages an all-or-nothing approach to life. It doesn't want you to do anything even remotely risky. So how can you get back in control and direct your own life? How can you use your thinking when your feelings are steering the car?

Reacting Versus Responding

In order to calm down, Monica had to begin to focus on herself instead of everyone else. I encouraged her to start paying attention to how her anxiety alarm was running the show in her day-to-day life. After some observation, Monica told me a story about a recent encounter with her boyfriend. He had texted her to say that he was locked out of his apartment. Monica had the spare key, but she had just gotten out of the shower and started cooking her dinner. She could feel the anxiety in his voice, because being locked out is pretty annoying. Unable to differentiate between her boyfriend's anxiety and reality, Monica quickly raced across town. Her hair was wet, her dinner was unfinished, and her coat wasn't warm enough. When she met him at a bar near his apartment, she noticed that he had calmed down. "You didn't have to rush over here," he said. "Your hair is frozen!"

Oversensitive to her boyfriend's anxiety, Monica was unable to stop and consider that he was perfectly capable of traveling across town to retrieve the key from her. The alarm had sounded, and she had responded like a true firefighter. But there was no fire!

Many of us are sneaky good at pretending that we aren't anxious creatures. We're usually not punching people in the face or screaming on the phone. We show up for work on time and pay our taxes. We tend to be subtle neurotics who take on too much or just really want people to like us. But the neuroses take their toll. The alarm sounds, and we end up reacting instead of responding. Reacting is your anxious response. And your anxiety wants you to act quickly and comfortably, even if it isn't a mature behavior. Responding looks like thinking and being the kind of person you want to be. Let's look at some examples of how people react or respond.

Reacting (feelings) can look like:
- answering nonemergency emails at ten p.m.
- not taking chances for fear of rejection
- setting impossible deadlines
- being overly accommodating to other people
- taking on responsibilities of no interest or value
- checking social media to see if people like your post

Responding (thinking) will look like:
- sharing your thinking without focusing on the reaction
- seeing rejection as manageable and inevitable

- setting realistic deadlines
- saying no to tasks not in line with your values and interests
- refraining from managing other people's emotions or behaviors

The difference in these two lists is the difference between a person with a low level of differentiation and a person with a higher level of differentiation. And you can take a wild guess which person will get more work done and be better at managing anxiety. Take a look at that first list again, and notice how the reactive person is other-focused. When we're reactive, we try to read people's minds. *Did they like my idea? Did they think I was too blunt? Should I send a second, nicer email?* When you try to read someone's mind, you're likely to assume the worst. You're going to let your anxiety dictate your reaction.

Living life as a series of anxious reactions is exhausting. When we inevitably feel overwhelmed with trying to look good and be loved, we use caffeine, alcohol, food, television, shopping, more achieving, and other people to calm ourselves down. Most of the time, people can get by with this kind of functioning. But the second a big wave of stress hits, like a death, a breakup, a job loss, or an illness, our sense of self will topple like the fragile structure that it is.

Post-topple is when most people show up to therapy. In twelve-step groups, this is called Step 1: "We admit that we are powerless over _____. Our lives have become unmanageable."

That blank space is whatever you have been doing to manage your anxiety. We're all addicted to some way of calming ourselves down, whether it's praise, or being busy, or booze. Step 1 is one way that people admit that their autopilot for calming themselves down really doesn't work.

For many of us, that blank space is the love and approval of others. Dr. Bowen challenged the idea that people who came to therapy feeling unloved needed more love. He saw them as being "addicted" to love. It wasn't that their parents didn't love them enough. It was that there was little emotional separation in their families. And with any addiction, more of the substance doesn't solve the problem. It just temporarily calmed things down, like obsessively refreshing Twitter or ordering another cocktail.

Like Monica, many people end up in therapy looking for assurance and approval. Remembering Dr. Bowen's words, I tried my best not to jump right into that role. Monica had to learn to calm herself down, and I couldn't do it for her. When she burst into tears, I didn't reassure her that everything was going to work out. I didn't offer her solutions when she insisted she had no idea what to do. Instead, I tried my best to communicate how interested I was in hearing her thinking. One session when she was on her tenth Kleenex, I looked at her and said, "I'm just so curious about how you're going to figure this stuff out." She could see that I was along for the ride, but that she was calling the shots. That her thinking was just as valuable as my own, if not more so. And you know what happened? She got interested in herself, too. Rather than beating herself up, she got curious about her behaviors and her anxiety. She kept a journal of her observations and was always eager to share them with me. She was perceiving her life with the curiosity of a researcher rather than the disapproval of a critic.

I truly believe that the opposite of anxiety is curiosity. If I can stay curious about my therapy clients, they will often do better. When I jump in and try to fix things for a client, I am communicating that they aren't capable of solving the problem themselves, that their thinking isn't useful and they should borrow mine instead. If I'm more concerned with calming everything down rather than letting a person take responsibility for themselves, I would be reacting instead of responding, and I would become just like Monica, trying to make everyone happy.

Armed with curiosity instead of guilt or shame, Monica started to notice when she jumped into anxious action. So she wouldn't forget to slow down and think, she hung up a giant sign in her bedroom that said, "There is no fire!" The sign made her laugh, and laughter is sometimes the best antidote to anxiety. Slowly, she was taking back the wheel. She still burst into tears when her boss sent her an email with negative feedback, but she chose to go for a run instead of complaining to another coworker. Her father became angry when she reconnected with her brother, but she began to believe that her father was wrong—there were no villains in her family. Her heart rate skyrocketed when a friend snapped at her, but she took deep breaths and held her ground instead of sending twenty apology texts.

Monica was starting to get a taste of being more differentiated, or what is called "being a self." She learned that progress isn't the absence of anxiety. It's the ability to choose how you respond to it and the ability to be mature when faced with it. Monica was choosing the life she wanted, and she chose a life in which disappointment, disagreement, and even failure were not just survivable; she chose a life in which she could thrive in the midst of them.

Your Questions

Observe

- When is it difficult to tease apart my thinking and my emotions?
- In what relationships is it difficult to differentiate my thinking from the thinking of others?
- When does my anxiety perceive danger where there is none?

Evaluate

- How does responding to imagined danger negatively affect my life?

- What kind of thoughtful responses would I like to have in anxious situations?
- What wisdom would I like to remember when I want to react instead of respond?

Interrupt

- How can I sit with the discomfort of not letting my autopilot manage my anxiety?
- How would I like to work on distinguishing between thoughts and emotions?
- What experiences or people do I need to seek out to work on differentiation?

Your Practice

Making friends with your anxiety means paying attention to the wacky things it will tell you. Try giving your anxiety a name (mine is called Carl), and write a letter to yourself from your anxiety. E.g., "Dear Kathleen, this is your anxiety. Let me tell you all the things that could go wrong today!" Read what it has to say, and then calmly write a letter back using your best thinking and focusing on the facts. When you become pen pals with your anxiety, you may find that your anxiety is just a nervous friend who really has your best interests at heart. But that doesn't mean that you should always listen to it.

CHAPTER 3

Your Pretend Self

Do I need to be liked? Absolutely not. I like to be liked. I enjoy being liked. I have to be liked, but it's not like this compulsive need to be liked, like my need to be praised.

—Michael Scott, The Office

Maybe you've been reading this book, and so far you've been thinking, "I've got it together, Kathleen. I'm pretty differentiated. My anxiety isn't running the show." Well then, TAKE A SEAT, SON. 'Cause we're about to get real. In this chapter, I'm going to talk about all the ways that we pretend we're fine. Because sometimes we're so good at exuding a fake calm, we can even fool ourselves.

Adam started therapy when Donald Trump became president. Not because he had Trump malaise like most of DC, but because he had lost his job when the administration changed. Adam was twenty-five and had chosen a career in politics after becoming enamored with *The West Wing*. He had gone to the best schools, snagged some killer internships, and landed a sweet job in the Obama administration. But Adam's success train flew off the rails when he had to leave his job on Inauguration Day in 2017. Months later, still unemployed, he struggled to get out of bed in the morning. He showered maybe twice a week, and he only felt good on days that his partner was around. Adam was depressed, and he couldn't seem to find the motivation to keep applying to jobs.

Any person encountering Adam at his old job would have seen an impressive, emotionally mature young man. A man who was capable of staying calm and thinking under pressure. So how did he end up overwhelmed with anxiety and covered in Dorito dust on the couch?

Let's go back to the concept of differentiation. When Dr. Bowen was thinking about what helped some people be more differentiated than others, he noticed that you couldn't exactly judge a person by their outward performance. People seemed to have two selves that influenced their functioning. There was a solid self that consisted of the person's true beliefs, values, and abilities. And then there was a pseudo-self, which is the part of the person that is negotiable. The pseudo-self is susceptible to relationship pressure—how you act depends on who's in the room. Maybe you are a capable leader at

PSEUDO-SELF BOOSTERS

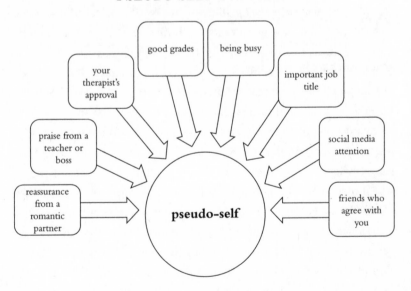

work, but you turn into a brat when your siblings are around. The pseudo-self also can make us seem more differentiated than we really are. It can fake maturity, strength, and even calmness.

Adam's daily functioning and his mood had been boosted by his accomplishments and his position as a White House employee. People back in his hometown treated him as if he were a rock star. His parents loved to brag about him. All of the titles, praise, and attention, or what I call pseudo-self boosters, kept him calm and capable. But when they went away, his functioning took a nose dive.

Pseudo-Self Boosters

When we use pseudo-self boosters to define ourselves, we put an enormous amount of power into the hands of others. It's only human to feel good when we get a promotion or ace a test, but these things don't necessarily build a more solid sense of self. They can lower anxiety, but only temporarily. So we end up needing more and more of them, as if they were a drug. This dependence on others is called "borrowing self." We are quick to borrow confidence and calmness from those around us when we can't generate it ourselves.

A certain amount of borrowing and lending of self happens in any relationship. We borrow calmness or capacity from others, and we lend it to them as well. But too much borrowing leaves us vulnerable to anxiety, depression, and other symptoms. When we give people the power to raise our functioning, we also give them the power to deflate us like a bouncy castle.

It's easy to assume that people with a high degree of professional or educational success have a higher level of differentiation. But like Adam, there are plenty of high-achievers whose moods will climb and plunge like a roller coaster with the presence or absence of praise or approval. Somebody with an admiring boss can skyrocket in their career, but when the boss leaves, they become depressed. A person's spouse can leave them, and their entire definition of self is gone. A straight-A student can graduate and find that they never developed the ability to be self-directed. We let so much of our self-worth be dependent on variables outside our control.

People often will come to therapy in distress because their pseudo-self has been running the show. A change or stressful event has occurred, and whatever propped up their sense of self-worth has disappeared. They discover that they don't have the ability to calm themselves or trust their own thinking. Though it can be tempting to rush out and find a shiny new person or accomplishment to make yourself feel better, this can be a perfect time to work on the ability to think for yourself and become more differentiated.

When I worked with Adam, we talked about what external variables he had used to boost his functioning. Adam saw how he used his partner's positive energy to gain pseudo-strength. He had used his job title and recognition from others to gain pseudo-importance. When he didn't have those, he began to use television and marijuana to calm his anxiety. But this only made him more depressed, and he wanted better ways of coping. Adam was aware of the fragility of his pseudo-self, and now he wanted to build a more solid one.

Like Adam, we all have ways of managing our fears of rejection, disappointment, and failure. For many people, especially overachievers, we bind up our anxiety by adhering to societal narratives about success. When we're operating in pseudo-self, our beliefs are negotiable, so we tend to adopt them from the culture around us. In American society, one of the most common narratives is that humans should operate like businesses. We should always be accomplishing more, increasing our income, and, at the very least, keeping up with our neighbors. We often don't take the time to use our own intellectual reasoning to consider whether that model is right for us or whether it's even realistic. But when we start to develop and test out some of our own thinking, our solid self begins to replace the functioning of the pseudo. We're standing on more solid ground.

Building Up Self

We often try to lower anxiety by seeking the *As—attention*, *assurance*, *approval*, and *agreement*. But when you stay focused on the reactions of others, your brain becomes pseudo-self territory. There is little space left for what you actually believe and value. To claim back that territory, you must put the focus back on yourself and learn to separate thinking from feeling. You must stay in contact with people but try not to depend on them too much for reassurance. When we reclaim the effort we put into seeking the *A*s, we suddenly have more energy to work on goals and self-soothe. We also enjoy our relationships more.

How to build up self instead of borrowing self:
- Breathe and relax your body before you respond to a challenge.
- Make a list of your possible choices or responses.
- Try to troubleshoot before you ask someone else to fix.
- Practice evaluating your own work before you ask for someone's opinion.
- Take time to define your own beliefs and values.

Once Adam could see where his pseudo-self was getting him into trouble, he began to keep the focus on himself and develop his own way of evaluating himself. He began to record his negative thoughts on a daily basis and observed an interesting theme. By thinking his unemployment made him worthless, Adam was borrowing from the world's definition of success. He certainly didn't believe that other people who didn't have impressive jobs were worthless. So why was he making himself the exception to the rule?

Adam decided he needed to outline a clearer definition of success. Because he was depressed, he needed a kinder and more objective way to evaluate his progress. So for the time being, he defined success as asking for help and taking care of himself. He summoned the courage to make an appointment with his psychiatrist, and he found that antidepressants helped keep his mood from fluctuating wildly. He recorded when he showered, when he got out of the house, and when he made it to the gym. That way when his anxiety told him that he wasn't doing anything, Adam could refer himself back to the list and stay focused on the facts. He also practiced managing his own distress before relying on his partner or his parents to reassure him that things were going to be okay.

Slowly but surely, Adam was learning that he didn't have to rely on other people's praise to know he was on the right track. He was perfectly capable of being objective, and he was realizing that his definition of the "right track" didn't have to play out like an Aaron Sorkin show. There would be times in life when he wouldn't get the attention he craved, but his mood and self-worth could survive and even thrive in them.

If you've spent a lot of time borrowing self from the people around you, you know that the highs of the praise roller coaster aren't worth the lows. If you're tired of pretending as if you have it together all the time, consider slowing down the chase of approval and taking time to define what's really important to you. Examine what definitions of success you've borrowed from the world without using your own brain. Consider how you've relied on other people's reactions to measure your self-worth. All of this can help you build a more solid sense of self. With a more solid self, you will be able to pursue your real passions, build authentic relationships, and know what you really believe in this anxious world.

Your Questions

Observe

- What achievements or people have I used to prop up my own mood and sense of self?
- When has my mood or functioning risen in the presence of pseudo-self boosters? When has it dropped?
- When have I focused more on seeking love and praise than developing my own beliefs and interests?

Evaluate

- How do I use approval or reassurance from others to manage my anxiety?
- When does my pseudo-self not reflect my actual beliefs and values?
- What wisdom would I like to remember when I want to use others to calm down?

Interrupt

- In what relationships and situations could I interrupt the "borrowing of self"?
- How can I take more responsibility for my own sense of self?
- How can I continue working on functioning with less pseudo-self?

Your Practice

Grab a piece of paper, and draw a brick wall. Label each brick with an achievement, title, or experience that has built up your sense of self.

Look at this structure, and ask yourself how many of these bricks are dependent on other people's responses to you. What bricks are filled with your intrinsic passions and interests? Running a 10K is totally within your control, but you can't control the number of people who like your Facebook post about the race. How can you begin to construct a self that is less focused on the recognition of others?

CHAPTER 4

Defining Yourself

> **Laws and principles are not for the times when there is no temptation: they are for such moments as this, when body and soul rise in mutiny against their rigour....If at my individual convenience I might break them, what would be their worth?**
>
> —*Jane in Charlotte Brontë's Jane Eyre*

The year Carmen turned thirty-five, she got a weird rash on her arm. She was too busy with her work to go to the dermatologist, so she just brushed it off. I mean *literally* brushed it off because that rash was flaky as hell. But then she started getting tired all the time, and she found more weird spots on her skin. When her hair started falling out, she freaked. Her doctor ran some tests, and soon enough, she learned that she had lupus.

When Carmen came to see me three years later, she didn't know if she had time for therapy. She worked a high-stress job in crisis management, and she wanted to spend her scant time with her partner and friends. But Carmen struggled to talk to people about her chronic illness. Since her diagnosis, being around her family was particularly anxiety-producing. Carmen had two parents and two older sisters, and she always fought with them when she went home for the holidays. "They treat me like

I'm helpless. My mother wants me to move back home to California. We can't go forty-eight hours without a shouting match."

Carmen also had avoided having an honest conversation with her boss about her diagnosis. She would arrive late to work on days she felt fatigued but lie about the reasons. "I don't want it to seem like I can't keep up," she said. "But I feel like my life is now a square peg that I'm trying to fit into a round hole. Something has to change. I don't want to get sicker because I can't slow down."

In Chapter 3, I talked about how people don't take the trouble to define themselves until their pretend self takes a hit. Often this happens when people experience a major unexpected life event. After a certain amount of stress, we can no longer get by with our automatic functioning. Have you started to think about all the ways that you've borrowed confidence or calm from other people? From addictions or distractions? How exactly does one construct a more solid sense of self?

By now you might be saying, "Please, Kathleen, just give me the tools!" People freaking love tools. People come to therapy, and the first thing out of their mouth is, "I need tools!" But if you're just borrowing solutions from me, then how is that any different? That's the thing about defining yourself—only you can do it—but I can tell you what it looked like for Carmen.

What Do You Really Believe?

Quiz time. Do you remember the two components of differentiation?
1. the ability to separate thoughts from feelings
2. the ability to separate these from other people's thoughts and feelings

There's an individual component and a relationship component to being a more differentiated person. So it makes sense that building a more solid self, one that's less susceptible to anxiety, would mean working on yourself and working on yourself *in relationships*. If you need a sports metaphor, think of it as first learning to hit a three-pointer and then making the shot with a person guarding you. You have to *think* like an individual, and then you have to *think and act* like an individual around other people. The second step is the real test, but you can't do it unless you've completed the first.

In the previous chapter, we talked about how your pseudo-self will adopt many beliefs and ideas from other people without thinking much about them. So to build a more solid self, you have to begin to think about what it is that you *actually believe*, not what you believe when it's convenient, or when it looks good, or when it's the opposite of whatever Ted at the office thinks because you hate that guy! True beliefs are not about conforming or rebelling. They're not about who's in the room. True beliefs are what you think, based on your own logic and reasoning.

When people start studying Bowen theory, they are often given the assignment of writing a "belief paper." A belief paper can be about any topic or many topics. The point is to get you to start thinking about what you value and believe based on your intellectual reasoning. When people start this kind of thinking, they often realize how little time they've dedicated to developing their own thinking. But the truth is, you can't have solid convictions or beliefs if they're not, well...SOLID. Flimsy or underdeveloped beliefs are going to succumb to the pressure of other people, which is sometimes called "groupthink."

Underdeveloped beliefs lead to:
- storming out of the room
- conforming to the group
- cutting off from people who disagree
- arguing with people
- trying to convince people
- more anxiety!

Having well-developed, solid beliefs doesn't mean that they're rigid or dogmatic. Many people will find that their beliefs will change based on new experiences, evidence, or knowledge. The key is that you're not just changing them to make other people happy or to calm them down. It's a thought-out process rather than an automatic one. Again, it's the difference between reacting and responding.

When people begin to work on their level of differentiation, they often want to fast forward to the part where you define your beliefs to others and stand your ground. But how can you do that if you haven't figured out what those beliefs are? This is where Carmen was when she came to meet with me. She wanted to be able to define herself to her family and to her boss, but she hadn't yet taken the time to develop her own thinking about living with lupus. She wasn't sure what it would look like to live her best life when it included a chronic illness. She didn't know what she believed, and thinking about it was even a little scary.

Here's the thing about defining your beliefs and values—you can't do it over lunch. It takes time. People are great at coming up with excuses for having no time to decide what they believe about marriage, their career, their passions, or their faith. But these are often the things we say are the most important to us. When people do sit down to think, often they will find that it's anxiety-producing. It's the opposite of staying busy or distracting yourself with Netflix. But remember, uncomfortable means you're off autopilot. It means you're shedding some of that pseudo-self skin.

Identifying Your Principles

Carmen began to think about how she wanted to live her life and what she really valued. She thought about what her best self would do in challenging situations. She focused on the facts of her illness and not the fantasy of being cured or the nightmare of hypothetical problems.

Over time, Carmen began to cultivate some reality-based wisdom she wanted to remember when she became anxious. She wrote down some guidelines to help keep herself off anxious autopilot—guidelines that were focused on long-term calm rather than short-term relief. In other words, she was functioning based on what she thought rather than how she felt.

Dr. Bowen called this "functioning based on principle." Here are the principles that Carmen came up with.

Carmen's Principles

- I will let my family know about my illness without trying to calm them down.
- I will speak up and be honest with my boss when I need more time.
- I will do one thing at a time instead of rushing through the day.
- I will prioritize my health over the desire to keep up with everyone else.
- I will accept care and help from my partner when necessary.

When she saw these written down, Carmen realized how much her principles were the exact opposite of her anxious behaviors. Her anxiety wanted her to reassure her family or avoid them. It told her to lie to her boss, rush through the day, self-compare, and refuse support. No wonder she had felt so overwhelmed. Looking at the list, she could also see the challenges ahead. It would be scary to do things she normally wouldn't do. But it would also be fascinating to see what happened.

At the back of this book, you'll find some space for you to start thinking about your guiding principles. Depending on your challenges and continued thinking, your principles may change over time. But it's useful to begin considering how you'd like to live your life differently. Principles can help you do the opposite of what your anxiety would have you do.

Defining Yourself in Relationships

Having principles sounds so fancy and mature, doesn't it? Some people hang them on their mirror or even memorize them. For a while, I kept mine taped to the back of my phone. But here's the challenge—you've got to follow your principles when other people are in the room. This is the true test of defining yourself. Because other humans will have their own thoughts and their own anxieties. Change doesn't happen in a vacuum. Change doesn't even really happen in therapy. You change *while in relationships* with the people closest to you. What does that mean?

It means you're never going to change if you're avoiding the people with whom you have the least emotional separation. The people who can really push your buttons. Do I need to spell it out? Y-O-U-R F-A-M-I-L-Y.

So now Carmen had the challenge of following her principles as a member of her family, an employee at her firm, and a partner in her romantic relationship. She was out of the locker room and on the court. And she was going to try not doing what she would normally do, which is argue with her mother or avoid her boss. In short, she was going to try to raise her level of differentiation.

When you go into relationships and try to do something different, people usually aren't going to like it. Your family or office doesn't want you to upset the balance they've cultivated to keep things calm. So when you change, there will be a temporary increase of anxiety in the system. Sometimes people will readjust quickly to your new behavior. But often, especially in highly anxious families, people will say, "What the hell are you doing? This is not how we do things! You're not yourself anymore. Please stop." Eventually, however, they will readjust to the new reality.

DEFINING YOURSELF

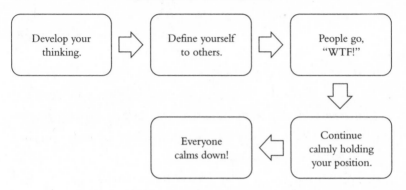

This is exactly what happened with Carmen. She went home for vacation, and she tried to be honest and open with her family. As expected, her mother followed her around the house, word-vomiting her anxiety all over Carmen. "How are you going to keep your job if you have to go to the hospital? Are you sure you don't want to move home? Is your insurance good enough?"

Carmen tried to follow her first principle: being honest without taking responsibility for her mother's emotions. She tried *so* hard! But like any child, she was highly allergic to her mother's anxiety. Finally, Carmen couldn't take it anymore and yelled at her mother. They both ended up in tears.

Learning to be a self in your family takes a lot of work. You're probably not going to get it right on the first try, or maybe even the tenth. But if you can make it a little bit longer without reacting each time, and keep increasing your capacity to think, then I call that a victory. And less reactivity around your family will easily translate to every other arena in life.

So Carmen kept training. Eventually, on another trip home, Carmen was able to stay calm when interrogated. She listened to her mother's concerns, and here is what she said:

"Mom, I am learning how to live with my lupus. I cannot teach

37

you how to live with a daughter who has lupus. You're going to have to figure out how to do that yourself."

Carmen didn't say this in a mean-spirited way. She simply shared her thinking with her mother.

Folks, this is what we call *being a self.*

Carmen had done it. She had stayed calm and shared her thinking. Internally, she felt balloons fall from the ceiling. So did her mom finally see the light and calm down? Did she say, "Thank you, Carmen. I needed to hear that."?

Lol. No. No, she did not. She accused Carmen of being cold. She said, "I don't even know you anymore!" She started crying. Whoa boy.

But Carmen was prepared. She knew that defining herself might prompt a strong reaction in her mother. But she couldn't expect her mom to understand her thinking so quickly. Her mom needed her own time to think and resettle in the new status quo. Waiting for this readjustment requires a lot of patience. It's so easy to jump back into immaturity when people react anxiously to our new way of functioning. But that's the true test of defining yourself.

With time, Carmen's mom calmed down. She started going to therapy, and she could talk about Carmen's illness without freaking out as much. She began to see that her daughter was capable, and she treated her like it. Similarly, Carmen kept treating her mom as if she were capable of handling herself.

This story has a happy ending. But defining yourself may mean that people aren't always going to love you for it or accept you. It does mean, however, that your sense of self will be less dependent on that acceptance. Plus, you'll have less anxiety. And like Carmen's family, people around you might calm down a little bit too. I love it when people calm down.

Your Questions

Observe

- When do I adopt beliefs or values from others without doing my own thinking?
- Where have my underdeveloped beliefs caused conflict or increased anxiety?
- In what relationships is it particularly difficult to think for myself or communicate my thinking?

Evaluate

- What are challenges in my life for which I'd like to develop some guiding principles?
- How can I make time to develop these principles?
- What people or resources can help me develop these principles?

Interrupt

- What behaviors would I have to interrupt to be a more differentiated person?
- What people would I need to increase contact with to practice defining myself?
- How can I prepare myself for the inevitable pushback when I define my thinking to others?

Your Practice

Imagine that aliens have crash-landed in your backyard. In exchange for giving you the secret to light-speed travel, they ask that you share your five wisest thoughts on being a mature human. What thinking would you share with them? Does this reflect how you operate in your relationships with other humans? Consider how you can make these operating instructions available to you in anxious times.

Let's Review Part 1!

We have covered a lot in these four chapters. Let's summarize what we've learned.

1. **Start focusing on yourself.** If you want to lower anxiety, you have to understand how you currently manage it. But anxiety wants us to stay focused on everyone else and what they're doing wrong. It wants us to ask questions like "Why?" so we can have someone or something to blame. The challenge is to start treating yourself like a research project and notice what you do to manage anxiety in yourself and in relationships.

2. **Practice separating your thinking from your feeling.** Anxiety is very good at distorting reality and making you sense imagined threats. Your level of **differentiation** is your ability to separate your thinking from your feeling, what's real from what's imaginary.

3. **Practice differentiating your thoughts and emotions from those of others.** Your level of differentiation is also your ability to separate how you feel and think from how others feel and think. People with lower levels of differentiation are less emotionally separated from their families, and they have a harder time thinking for themselves.

4. **Observe how you borrow functioning from others.** The **pseudo-self** is the part of your functioning that is changeable based on relationships with others. Our pseudo-self can rely on external variables to create an appearance of strength,

importance, or calmness; this puts our functioning and our mood in the hands of others, which keeps us vulnerable to stress.

5. **Begin to define your beliefs and principles.** People who are working on their level of differentiation will begin to more fully develop their beliefs and guiding principles. They are willing to refrain from doing what they automatically do to manage their anxiety and direct themselves by their own thinking.

6. **Practice defining yourself in significant relationships.** This practice of **defining self** happens through contact with significant people in your life. Defining oneself may temporarily increase anxiety, but over time it will lower chronic anxiety in yourself and the relationship.

These steps aren't linear and then BOOM you're done. Calming down involves a lifelong process of observing, evaluating, and interrupting over and over again. You can never underestimate the necessity of continual observation. It is the call to know thyself that truly calms you down. So that's what we're going to do in the next section of the book. We're going to get more specific about the predictable ways that humans manage anxiety in their relationships. We'll talk about your parents, your boo, your friends, and your community. Ready to be less anxious around all of those lovely people?

Part Two

* * *

YOUR ANXIOUS
RELATIONSHIPS

CHAPTER 5

Your Family

> I think a dysfunctional family is any family with
> more than one person in it.
>
> —*Mary Karr*, The Liars' Club

Richard came to therapy with an interesting predicament: he had a family. By any other measure, Richard was busting all the myths of the struggling millennial. He held an exciting position with a digital strategy firm. He had avoided costly avocado toast and thereby saved enough money to buy a condo. His relationship with his boyfriend of two years was going strong, and he was getting ready to propose. But there was one tiny issue—Richard's family was anxious about his sexuality, and he had yet to introduce his boyfriend to them.

To an outsider, Richard's family gave off a convincible façade of calmness. His parents were retired and living in South Carolina. His younger brother, Kevin, had spent the last seven years dabbling in college and bouncing back and forth between his parents' basement and rehab. His older sister, Katherine, got along with everyone by living thousands of miles away in California. And his grandma ruled the family from her Iron Throne, an assisted living facility down the street from his parents. Just your typical All American Family.

Everyone in Richard's family had come to the unspoken agreement that keeping Grandma happy and solving Kevin's problems were the best ways for everyone to get along. Richard broke the first rule when he had come out to his parents in college. There was no yelling, but there was no hugging either. Just an anxious, "We love you, but have you considered that this might prematurely kill your grandmother?" Richard's parents were lapsed evangelicals, so he was never certain of what they believed about human sexuality. But he did know that avoiding family drama was more important to them than anything else. So his best strategy for keeping them calm was to tell his grandmother that he hadn't found the right girl yet. But now a wedding was on the horizon, and he wanted everyone in his family to be there. Avoiding the subject no longer seemed like an option.

Your Family Is an Anxiety-Managing Machine

If you've been paying attention so far, you'll remember that humans have built-in responses to anxiety in order to survive. We spend a lot of time mentally beating ourselves up for these responses, and we benefit when we simply observe them and ask ourselves whether we might like to add some different, more mature behaviors to our repertoire.

But when you only focus on individual behavior, you miss the bigger picture. We don't live in a vacuum. We're social creatures, and we're constantly reacting to other humans. In Part 1 of the book, we looked at how to focus on yourself. But in Part 2, you're going to zoom out and practice focusing on yourself in the context of these larger relationship systems. Like our individual selves, these larger systems are also doing their best to manage anxiety and keep things relatively calm.

The most basic relationship system is your family. Why do we have families? Why don't we just emerge fully formed and ready to go, like thousands of tiny seahorses exploding out of the belly of their father? That would be awesome. Unfortunately, we can't survive on our own at birth, and we need our fellow humans to solve problems and manage stress. Most of us think that our families are factories that churn out anxiety, but the truth is that they are built to reduce anxiety. Families are anxiety-managing machines, and they do this remarkably well most of the time.

If you want to be an expert observer of your own anxious behaviors, you have to look at the way your family functions, or what Dr. Bowen called the emotional process. Fortunately, you don't need a degree in family therapy to do this. Families are notoriously uncreative in how they manage stress. There are really only a couple of strategies they use, and once you learn them, they're easy to spot. Seeing these strategies can help you be a little bit freer to choose how you want to act, even when your sister "borrows" your car or your mother asks you if you'll be single forever. Let's take a look at them.

Strategy #1: Distance

Avoiding people like the plague continues to be the most common strategy in every family for dealing with anxiety. This distance could be physical, like when Richard's sister moved across the country or his decision to only come home once a year. But it can also be a lack of real communication, known as emotional distance. Richard was emotionally distant from his grandmother, because he never talked about his personal life, and from his brother, because they only talked about college basketball.

Here are some other ways that you might use distance to manage anxiety in your family:
- sticking to superficial conversation topics
- emailing or texting instead of talking in person
- planning a full schedule to keep everyone busy
- keeping the TV on at family gatherings

- working long hours
- drinking or getting high

What's important to note is that distance isn't good or bad. It's a force that's always present, and we wouldn't use it if it didn't work really damn well a lot of the time. Who among us hasn't pretended to be fascinated by football at Thanksgiving or poured a shot before a cousin's bar mitzvah? But at some point, we may have to interact with people who make us anxious. We may have to talk about tough decisions instead of how much rain we've gotten. We have to turn off *The Price Is Right* and tell Grandpa that we're not going to business school. Sometimes we need to tell people what we think and believe, what's really important to us, or who we really are. And if we've only been using distance, then our capacity to deal with this anxiety is going to be pretty low.

When you practice being less distant with family, you begin to immunize yourself a little more against anxiety. Do you know what happens when you get a vaccine? Often you get a little dose of the disease in weakened form, so that your body will begin producing antibodies. You are put into contact with the disease so that you are better prepared to handle it in the future. So if it's helpful to think of your boring aunt as a case of rotavirus, then by all means go for it.

Richard used distance as a way of managing the anxiety surrounding his sexual orientation. He didn't go home that often, and when he talked to Grandma, it was always about the weather or his work. Richard wanted to be less insecure when it came to talking about his personal life, but he wasn't getting a lot of practice. He'd only bring it up around his parents when his sister could be a buffer. In order to calm down, he was going to have to temporarily increase the anxiety by sharing about his life. To be more of a self in his family, he was going to have to work on his one-to-one relationship with everyone, including his grandmother.

Strategy #2: Conflict

At first glance, fighting seems like a way of causing anxiety rather than managing it. But think about it. Human families have had thousands of years to evolve, and we're still feuding over who gets Great Aunt Mary's lamp. So we must get something out of conflict, right?

Conflict can temporarily calm you in an anxious situation. If I am convinced that you are wrong, and that you are the person who needs to change, then I can relax a little bit. I might feel less insecure. Suddenly I feel as if I've got it together, and you're the one who needs to go to therapy. Seriously, go to therapy, Brenda!

If you ask someone what causes conflict in a family, you'll get a few common answers:

- religion
- politics
- money
- sex

You might have a hard time believing this in our current social and political climate, but these topics don't necessarily cause conflict. It's the emotional reactivity, or what Dr. Bowen called immaturity, that we bring to these subjects that allows for conflict to arise. To reduce conflict, we don't have to get everyone to agree. We simply have to manage our reactivity. In short, you have to be more mature, and switch off that autopilot that makes you extend your claws.

In addition to sexuality, money was a topic that brought out the immaturity in Richard's family. Richard and his sister, Katherine, wanted their parents to stop giving their younger brother, Kevin, money, because they believed it supported his addiction. They also thought it was unfair to them, because they had stayed out of trouble and gotten squat. On the other side of the conflict, Richard's parents were worried their child would wind up in the morgue if he wasn't safe in their basement. Stuck in the middle of this conflict, Kevin simply disappeared whenever the subject came up. So you can imagine how many emotions were brought to these conversations—fear, anger, embarrassment, frustration, and jealousy were all present, and they kept everyone from calming down and solving the problem.

To refrain from jumping into conflict, Richard would have to be able to do two things. He'd have to pay attention to how everyone reacted anxiously when the subject of money came up. He'd also have to observe how his own immaturity helped perpetuate the conflict, rather than simply blaming his parents or brother for making bad decisions.

Strategy #3: Triangles

Families are tangled webs of communication. When tension is high between two people, it spills over into other relationships. We pull people into the conflict, wanting allies, confidantes, and messengers. When we use a third person to manage anxiety or tension, this is called a triangle. Triangles are so common in families that once you begin to look for them, you'll realize they're everywhere.

Triangles can look like:
- gossiping about someone
- venting your frustrations
- asking someone to relay messages
- asking someone to gather information
- taking sides in an argument
- bringing a buffer to a gathering

Richard's family was full of triangles. Katherine would call him when she was fighting with their mom. His grandmother would ask him to talk to Kevin about finishing college. Richard would try to convince his parents to tell Grandma that he was gay. Everywhere you looked, people were using others as a go-between to avoid difficult conversations. They relied on triangles when one-to-one relationships were weak, distant, or difficult.

The more stress there is in a family, the more triangles are activated. Richard noticed that he was in a triangle with his mom and sister regarding his romantic life. He would grow angry when his mother said something inconsiderate. He'd text his sister to complain, and she would leave an angry voicemail for their mother. Around and around they went—the triangle was a Band-Aid that didn't help anyone become more mature.

THE TRIANGLE

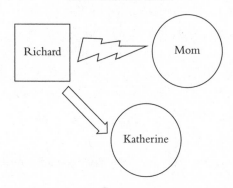

Strategy #4: Overfunctioning and Underfunctioning

Often in anxious families, one person will take on more responsibility when another person seems less capable. This results in a sort of seesaw dynamic known as overfunctioning and underfunctioning. It often happens in marriages, but children can also overfunction for their parents, or siblings for one another. The underfunctioner gets labeled as the problem spouse or the problem child, but everyone plays a part in this dynamic.

The truth is, sometimes it's just easier to do something for someone than it is to watch them attempt a task. If you don't believe me, then clearly a parent has never asked you to help them set up any piece of technology. It's also easier to feign helplessness when there's someone who can just do things for you. After all, why should you learn to do your taxes when it brings Dad such joy? It's amazing how the presence of another family member can trigger these different responses.

Richard could look at his family and see how his mother was often the overfunctioner. She was a tornado of a woman, constantly cleaning and feeding everyone. She filled out job applications for Kevin when he claimed he didn't have the energy. She lectured everyone on what to tell Grandma and when they should just lie to her. Richard admitted that it was easier to underfunction, letting his mother call the shots. Other times he mimicked his mother, treating his brother and father as if they were less capable.

Looking at all of the strategies his family used to manage anxiety, Richard saw his family functioning like a game of Twister. Everyone was reaching over and around another, and it wouldn't take much to knock the whole thing over.

Calming Down Around Your Family

Understanding these four strategies can help you see your family as an anxiety-managing machine. The more you observe distance, conflict, triangles, and over/underfunctioning as natural and even adaptive responses to anxiety, the harder it becomes to blame your family or label someone as the problem or the villain. And when there are no villains, you will feel less reactive and act more neutral. You'll understand that everyone plays a part in the family drama, and the only part you can control is you. If you change one variable, you change the whole equation.

Richard and I talked about how he could observe his family more if he started calling more often and taking more frequent trips home. He didn't need to do anything different at first—he simply needed to pay attention and take some notes. After one such trip, here's what he noticed:

Distance: I distance from my grandmother by not mentioning my personal life.

Conflict: I promote conflict by telling my parents they must stop giving Kevin money.

Triangles: I create a triangle when I vent to my sister about my parents.

Overfunctioning/Underfunctioning: I overfunction when I lecture my brother. I underfunction when I ask Mom to talk to Grandma for me.

I can't overstate how important observation is when it comes to lowering anxiety in your family. Often people will jump in and try to change themselves (or others!) without getting a good sense of how their family functions. The truth is you can't really lower your reactivity in your family, at least not with sheer willpower. But observation triggers that uniquely human front part of your brain, which overrides those instincts to fight, freeze, flee, or fret.

By taking the time to interact with his family, observe the emotional process, and list his observations, Richard had a road map for working on his anxiety and being a more differentiated person in his family. He simply had to stay in contact with people and *not do* what he would normally do.

Richard's Family Principles
- **Bridge Distance:** I can try to be open with my grandmother about my relationship and not manage her reaction, whatever it is.

- **Reduce Conflict:** I can try to be more neutral when my family disagrees about how to help Kevin. I can listen to what everyone thinks and then share my own thinking as well.
- **Avoid Triangles:** I can try to build a one-to-one relationship with every person in my immediate family, rather than gossiping or venting my frustrations to Katherine.
- **Function for Myself:** I can try to step back and let people take responsibility for themselves. I can also try to take responsibility for myself when it's tempting to let my mom or Katherine do things for me.

This list is pretty freaking mature. None of these tasks are simple. If you remember Carmen's story from Chapter 4, you know that changing your behavior will cause a temporary increase in anxiety before things ultimately calm down. Richard's mother might bristle at his refusal to manage Kevin. If he came out to Grandma, she might slam down the phone and stop calling him to talk about the pollen count. But Richard was ready to shake things up.

Shouldn't Some People Just Avoid Their Terrible Families?

When people learn about Bowen theory, one of their first objections is that there are some people whom you just shouldn't have in your life. The idea of increasing contact with them sounds unhealthy or even dangerous.

But these ideas aren't about telling people what they should do with their family. They are about interrupting what's automatic so that people can choose what to do. Often people think they are making a conscious choice when in reality they are replaying multigenerational patterns. When they look at their family history, they realize that cutting off contact or feuding has happened over and over again.

Richard looked at his family history and saw many examples of how relatives who had different beliefs from the family norms had fallen off everyone's radar. He knew that several of his mother's siblings no longer spoke with his grandmother. Seeing this history, Richard decided that he didn't just want to be another lost figure in his family. Though his grandmother and parents were frustrating, he didn't feel unsafe with them. Kevin could be exasperating, but he was a fun and decent human. Richard decided that he appreciated their presence in his life, and he could see value in working on being the most mature person in the room.

And that, my friends, is the definition of differentiation: being inside of your family and a little outside of the emotional process at the same time. You can be a part of your family without being on autopilot. You can choose how to respond with less reactivity. It's hard work, but it starts by learning to not be so surprised when families do what they always do.

A Little Bit of Freedom

Richard and his family didn't have some Hollywood ending in which everyone becomes insightful and unrecognizable. I imagine that they are still distancing, fighting, triangling, and over/underfunctioning like the rest of us, especially when stress is high. Richard's marker for success was simply to be a little freer of these processes. So every time Richard picked up his phone to call home or flew back for a visit, he reminded himself that he wasn't responsible for how anyone in his family behaved. He was responsible for being himself, being mature, and sharing what he wanted to share. And he wanted to share his boyfriend with Grandma because he loved them both. So that's what he did. And marvelously, over time, she calmed down about it. She was able to welcome Richard's now fiancé into her imperfect family.

Richard also worked hard to develop a relationship with his

brother that wasn't one strictly built on worry and overfunctioning. He began to treat Kevin as if he were a capable adult whose life wasn't going to implode at any moment. They grew closer, and Kevin benefitted from having at least one person in his family who was curious rather than fearful about how his life would turn out.

Surprisingly, Richard had the hardest time with Katherine. She wasn't thrilled when he started being more patient with their parents and less willing to vent about them with her. She became jealous as he grew closer to Kevin, accusing him of neglecting their relationship. But because Richard could look at their ongoing sibling triangle, he was less surprised by Katherine's reaction. He was able to stay calm with her even when she snapped at him.

Not every story about working on yourself in your family, especially when it comes to sexual orientation, will end the way Richard's did. Some families will never budge or will show hostility, and a person must evaluate how they want to respond to this challenge. The goal isn't to change people—it's to begin to choose your actions and not be swept up in the automatic processes.

Working on yourself in your family doesn't appeal to everyone. It doesn't fit with the quick-fix, solution-focused therapy that insurance companies love. For one thing, it takes time. People often want to work on their relationship with their romantic partner. Or they want to do breathing exercises or journal positive affirmations. But spend more time with their family? Call that weird relative? No thank you.

But I truly believe that working on yourself in your family makes the biggest difference in your anxiety level. When Olympic athletes train at higher altitudes, they are faster and stronger when they compete. Your family is high-altitude training for anxiety: if you can be calmer in your family, you can do it anywhere—at work, on the subway, on a date, or when you're by yourself.

Your Questions

Observe

- When does my family use distance, conflict, triangles, or over/ underfunctioning to deal with anxiety or tension?
- When and how do I participate in these strategies?
- What one-to-one relationships are my weakest in my family?

Evaluate

- When do my behaviors in my family not reflect my best self?
- How do I see myself operating with more maturity in my family?
- What guiding principles would I like to remember the next time I visit my family?

Interrupt

- Where do I see upcoming opportunities for me to practice maturity in my family?
- How will I remind myself to zoom out and see the family as a system rather than blame individual people?
- How can I keep track of my progress as I work on family relationships?

Your Practice

In this chapter, you learned how families use anxiety-managing strategies, such as distance, conflict, triangles, and over/underfunctioning. Choose one of these strategies, and jot down a few examples of how your family has used this strategy to keep things calm. Now take a moment and consider what is the cost of using this strategy. Have triangles kept people from having one-to-one relationships? Has distance prevented people from sharing their true selves? Consider what an alternative to this way of functioning might look like and what kind of changes this would require from you. Remember, you can change how a family functions by changing yourself.

CHAPTER 6

Your Parents

> My mother—she was here. I can feel it. Smell that?
> The room—it smells like guilt and Chanel No. 5.
>
> —Lorelai, *Gilmore Girls*

Grace silenced her phone and slipped it back into her bag. "It's my mom. She always wants to know if I'm talking about her in therapy." We both laughed. Who doesn't talk about their mother in therapy?

Grace hadn't come to counseling because she wanted to work on her relationship with her mother. She'd had two panic attacks in the last month, both after fights with her boyfriend. She would hop in the shower to cry it out, and then WHAM! At first she thought she was having a heart attack. After two midnight trips to the emergency room, Grace decided that this was no way to live.

My client was symptom-focused, and for a good reason. Panic attacks are very unpleasant, as is the fear of having another one. But I was also interested in being systems-focused with Grace. I wanted to know more about her family, that anxiety-managing organism from which she came. Not to find someone to blame, but to understand more about her anxious autopilot and how she functioned in the world.

Grace was an only child, and her parents lived on the West Coast. Her father was a high school principal, her mother a real estate agent. They had divorced when she was a toddler, and Grace had grown up primarily with her mother. But she had followed in her father's footsteps and was working hard as an assistant principal at an elementary school.

Thousands of miles didn't keep Grace and her mother from constantly texting and talking. She explained to me that she felt chained to her phone. "My mom never tells me to have fun or to enjoy a trip. She just says, 'Be careful!' That's our family motto. If I don't call her the minute my plane lands, or text her when I get home late, she blows up my phone. She always expects me to get mugged or die in a fiery crash."

Grace's mother wasn't the only one doing an anxious dance. Grace described her mother as having an "addictive personality." Her compulsive shopping had left her with massive credit card debt, and her eating habits had led to type 2 diabetes. Grace was terrified that her mother would die and leave her, or end up broke and want to move in with her. They were caught in an endless cycle of worrying and lecturing, and neither seemed interested in doing much changing.

The Original Relationship

For most of us, our relationship with our parents (or primary caregivers) is the first important relationship we have as humans. It's not surprising that many psychotherapy theories take a hard look at the early developmental stages in our life and how we bonded (or didn't bond) with our parents. But there's no need to go all Freudian when it comes to parents. If one or both of yours are still living, then simply observing how you interact with them can tell you just as much if not more than trying to recall your childhood. Real-time observation is much more accurate than memory.

Working on your relationship with a parent is the hardest work you can do, because you've had a lifetime to get locked into patterns with them. Many people come to therapy wanting to work on romantic relationships, friendships, or even work relationships before they will touch a parental one with a ten-foot pole. But going back to that primary relationship can make the biggest difference when we're trying to be a little calmer and a little more mature. It will have a positive impact on every other relationship in your life. You can get a new job or a new significant other, but you cannot trade your mom in for Cher or your dad for someone who doesn't use emojis. So you might as well take a look and see if some tinkering around might help you calm down a little.

Stop Parenting Your Parents

In addition to her panic attacks, Grace came to therapy because she couldn't decide whether she wanted to break up with her boyfriend, Eric. She was tired of always emptying the dishwasher and footing the Wi-Fi bill, while Eric drowned out her complaining with fantasy football podcasts. But Grace was wise enough to know that she was part of the equation when it came to a string of dud relationships—she tended to play caregiver while she dated guys who were happy to act helpless.

Grace could work on being less of an overfunctioner in her relationship with Eric, but if she wanted to break up with him, that was absolutely her prerogative. Her mother, on the other hand, wasn't going anywhere. Grace had never considered that her "parenting" in romantic relationships reflected her dynamic with her mother. Perhaps if she could learn to sit back and let her mom be more independent, it might be easier to stop mothering her boyfriends.

Frequently my clients will tell me stories of how they try to parent their parents. A young woman lets her mother call her for dating advice.

A financially successful man starts co-signing loans for his father, who struggles to manage money. The more your parents are overinvolved in your own life, the easier it is for you to return the favor.

Many adults who are focused on managing their parents have little energy left to pursue their own goals or manage their own anxiety. We can easily become people who try to teach our parents how to be healthy, manage money, and even navigate romantic relationships, while our own life is a dumpster fire. We love to fill in the maturity gaps of others before we address our own.

Some cultures place high value on caring for parents. Children are expected to start supporting their parents the second they become financially independent. And we should never label a cultural difference as a sign of immaturity. For me, anxiety is the barometer. Is taking care of your parents a thoughtful choice or an anxious, automatic one? Is the action based on principles and values, or is it you just trying to calm them down or prevent conflict? When we don't see the anxiety underneath the choice, we miss the point entirely.

When people end up overfunctioning for their parents, they fight a lot. This is because people really don't like to be managed or controlled. Often things will calm down when a person can develop their thinking about what it means to be an adult son or daughter. We think a lot about how to be a good partner or a capable employee, but seldom do people sit down and consider what it means to be an adult who has a parent in the world.

Grace was very focused on helping her mother learn to manage her diabetes. She'd interrogate her mother about her blood sugar levels and text her links to local gyms. Usually these conversations ended in tears or yelling. Grace was trying to manage her fears about her mother's health by attempting to control her. She directed, lectured, and downright begged, with little success. So she was ready to try something different.

One week for her therapy homework, I asked Grace to take a piece of paper and make two columns. In the first column, she would list what she felt were her responsibilities as an adult daughter. The second column would contain whatever she knew was not her responsibility. She came up with two interesting lists. She admitted that when it came to her mother's health, her sole duties were to listen and be supportive. And that was it! END OF LIST. She listed "giving advice" under the column of tasks that were not her tasks. Grace knew that she had to take responsibility for her own distress, and not her mother's.

If you're at risk of parenting your parent, it can be useful to sit down and clearly define your responsibilities in the relationship. Here are a few common answers.

Responsibilities of an Adult Child:
- being in regular contact
- taking time to listen
- sharing about my life
- treating my parents as if they're capable
- sharing my thinking when asked

A funny thing happened when Grace stopped trying to manage her mother's health and started to manage her own anxious reactions. Suddenly her mom had some breathing room to think about how she wanted to live a healthier life. When you can get a clearer sense of what your role is with your parents and what it isn't, you might find that both you and your parents chill out a bit. Everyone is freer from the cycle of riling each other up and calming each other down.

Time to Grow Up!

As much as we may overfunction for our parents, we also will sometimes act like their children. Isn't this okay? Well, that depends—are you a child? Harsh, I know. It's easy to assume a position of helplessness—to underfunction—in times of anxiety. And many adults may have parents who are more than willing to swoop in and rescue them when they're distressed. When you're continually being rescued, you must ask yourself, "How is my acting helpless keeping me from being a more resilient person? How is it contributing to my own insecurities?"

Grace could look at her phone history and see how contacting her mom became her immediate response to distress. If her boss was being a jerk, or her boyfriend ditched her for friends, then she would shoot a whiny text to her mom. She knew that she always had an ally in her mother. This automatic response had kept Grace from being able to develop her own thinking about who she wanted to be at work and in her relationships. And her mother was more than willing to take on that role—it was comforting to her to know what was going on with her daughter 24/7. They each played a part in the dance of dysfunction, and one of them had to budge.

It was easy for Grace to act like a teenager or even a small child when she interacted with her mother. She didn't like herself when this younger version took control, and she didn't think it reflected who she wanted to be. Dr. Bowen taught that there is an adult and an infant inside of each of us, but the infant doesn't have to run the show. Remember in Chapter 3, when you learned about your pseudo-self? When we act helpless, or less capable, in the presence of another, then that is the pseudo-self acting like an infant. This happens often when we interact with our parents.

The infant will:
- act helpless
- blame others
- whine
- attack when criticized

- wait for the other to change
- struggle to think flexibly

But the adult can:
- take responsibility for herself
- self-soothe
- see the bigger picture
- hear different opinions
- model maturity
- think flexibly and objectively

When you become an adult, you're on a level playing field with everyone else who's an adult, including your parents. You are equally responsible for yourself and for modeling maturity in relationships. In other words, *no excuses*. If your mom is immature or mean, or your dad is an anxious mess, then you can no longer blame them for your own functioning. It's your job now to change how you operate in the world. You may also find that when that inner infant can take a backseat in your relationships with parents, you'll begin to feel more secure and act more capable at work, with a partner, and with friends.

Your Parents Are People

We all have fantasies of who or how we would like our parents to be. But I'm here to tell you that the Obamas aren't coming to adopt you, and your father isn't going to throw away his cargo shorts. When we use the fantasy as a measure, we miss the reality of having a relationship with our parents. One of the biggest challenges of adulthood is beginning to see your parents as people. While it's true that being a parent is a big part of someone's life, it's not the only part. Your parents have hopes, fears, and interests that have nothing to do with you. Shocking, I know.

Part of growing up means learning to be emotionally separate from our parents, by not letting their anxiety affect us as much. The people with the least emotional separation from their parents are the ones who struggle the most to see them as individuals. They usually respond by being extremely close to Mom or Dad or staying as far away from them as possible.

When you can't treat a parent like a person, it also becomes difficult to understand and relate to their choices. Grace was constantly questioning her mother's diet, spending habits, and the men she dated. Because she didn't treat her mother like a separate person, it was almost impossible for her to imagine that her mother would make choices she wouldn't make. Yet she dated weirdos, bought questionable real estate, and even wore socks with sandals.

Grace knew it wasn't her job to police her. But she struggled to keep her mouth shut when her mother became enamored with a sketchy dude or called her from Krispy Kreme. To help her stay neutral, we practiced creating some calm, supportive phrases she could use when she was tempted to manage her mother.

Don't say: Why are you spending all your time with that loser?
Try saying: It seems like you're very excited about this relationship!

Don't say: Can you please stop emailing me MapQuest directions? It's the twenty-first century!
Try saying: Thanks, but I'm going to use my phone to navigate.

Don't say: Taking the top off of your Egg McMuffin does not make it a healthy breakfast!
Try saying: It's great that you want to take care of yourself. I'm rooting for you!

Learn Your Family History

How do you begin to see Mom or Dad as a human and not your bumbling employee? I often encourage clients to begin to learn more about their family history. Going back a generation will help a person understand the forces that shaped their parents and the challenges they faced in their own immediate families. When she only focused on her nuclear family, Grace saw her mother as incompetent, anxious, and meddlesome. To gain more objectivity, we went back a generation.

Grace told me that her mother's father had died from a brain aneurysm when he was only forty-five years old. Her mother was the youngest in her family and was doted on by Grace's grandmother, who never remarried. When I asked about her mother's siblings, Grace explained that she didn't know them. Her mom had cut off contact with them after a dispute about her grandmother's estate.

By looking to the past, Grace was starting to see how her mother's experiences affected how she functioned. She no longer seemed controlling or vindictive. It made sense that a woman who had experienced a sudden death would worry a lot about her daughter. And it wasn't surprising that a woman who cut herself off from her family would be so anxiously focused on her daughter—there was nowhere else for her attention to go. Grace was able to see how her mother functioned, for better or worse, in response to these events. She was taking her anxiety-goggles off and seeing this woman for the first time.

Objectivity, however, doesn't always equal radical change. Grace could have this kind of clarity about her mother in therapy, but she struggled to think when her mom was harassing her on the phone. Her mom would say something she didn't like, Grace would snap back, and then one of them would hang up. Things would calm down, and then they'd start talking again. Grace tried withholding certain information about her relationship with her boyfriend to prevent her mom from getting upset or giving her unwanted advice, but this only made her mother more reactive.

I asked Grace if she had any pictures of her mother as a young girl. She said that she did, and we discussed how they could be visual reminders that she wasn't just her mother—she was a person with hopes and fears. We came up with the plan that she would look at that picture whenever she felt frustrated by her mother's constant contact. By keeping the picture in view, she could see the history of a woman trying her best to adapt to challenges and to tragedy. It was still difficult not to fight, but the photos helped her slow down and think. If she wanted her mother to treat her like an individual, then she'd have to do the same.

What If I'm Just Not Close with My Parents?

Many of my clients explain that they simply aren't close with their parents. Grace made this argument when I began to ask more about her father. He had remarried when she was little and had two more children who were much younger than Grace. She felt like a fifth wheel in his cute family of four, and her dad didn't make many moves to include her. She'd spend a few hours over the holidays with him, and she'd call when she needed career advice. But their conversations were peppered with awkward pauses, and she was quick to find excuses to hang up or leave. Besides, her mother scheduled Grace's time at home and would get jealous if she spent too much time at her dad's.

In Chapter 5, you learned how distancing is a common way we manage anxiety in our families. But people often misunderstand the goal of bridging distance with their parents—it's not to become best friends, to make them understand you better, or even to get their support. The goal is to learn to be more of an individual in this primary relationship. You move closer in order to become more separate. It sounds paradoxical, but think about it. The less affected you are by their anxiety, the greater capacity you have to develop a fulfilling relationship with them.

Starting a New Family Tradition

Grace was learning to be more objective about her parents, through observation and learning about her family history. She was also beginning to see her behavioral patterns in these relationships. She no longer saw herself as a victim of her mother's intenseness and her father's aloofness. If she could blame her parents, then they could just blame theirs. Where did it end?

She decided that she wanted to start new family traditions of openness and calmness. She wanted to be less reactive around her mother and less distant with her father. By changing herself, she would begin to change her family tree. Grace scheduled a weekly time when she would call her father. She prepared herself for awkward pauses as they talked more and learned about each other. Rather than waiting for an invitation, she shared her desire to spend more time with him and her siblings. They made plans for the holidays, and he finally booked a flight to come visit her in DC.

She also began to set some boundaries with her mother. She told her that she wanted to share about her life, but she was no longer going to call her every time her plane landed or she got home safe. Predictably, Grace's mother gave her a lot of pushback for taking this position. It would take time, but slowly she would learn that her daughter was a responsible adult who could take care of herself.

She also noticed that her mother had a few surprises for her. When she backed off lecturing her about money, boyfriends, or blood sugar, she noticed that her mother's brain was doing more of the work. She would never be a fitness guru or leave Grace a huge inheritance, but she was starting to listen more to her doctor and cut up her credit cards. The changes reminded Grace that her mother had been an intelligent adult this whole time.

Another funny thing happened as a result of Grace's work on her relationships with her parents. She began to notice that she got into fewer fights with her boyfriend. She stopped trying to manage him, the way her mother managed her, and she treated him like a capable adult. She now understood that this was perhaps the best gift you could give someone you loved.

Your Questions

Observe

- When do I become reactive when interacting with my parent(s)?
- How do I overfunction for my parent(s)?
- When does my inner infant take over in my relationship with my parent(s)?

Evaluate

- What are my responsibilities as an adult child of my parent(s)?
- How has my relationship with my parent(s) shaped how I interact with others?
- What might it look like to develop a less reactive and more mature relationship with my parent(s)?

Interrupt

- What are upcoming opportunities for me to practice being less reactive around my parent(s)?

- How can I refrain from reverting to automatic behaviors in these relationships?
- How can I remember that my parents are people who exist outside of their relationship with me?

Your Practice

If you want to be more like an adult and less like an infant around your parent, it can be helpful to have some neutral, nonjudgmental responses banked away when you're tempted to lecture, criticize, or whine. When your mom says she wants to start an Etsy shop selling crocheted fanny packs, try saying, "You seem so excited about this! I'm happy for you," instead of, "That's insane—what is wrong with you?" Take a few minutes to make a list of neutral replies that you can have handy when you need them. Remember, you don't have to agree with anything your parent says—you just have to remember that you're not responsible for managing their life.

CHAPTER 7

Ugh, Dating

> **Elaine: So basically what you're saying is that 95 percent of the population is undateable?**
> **Jerry: *Undateable!***
> **Elaine: Then how are all these people getting together?**
> **Jerry: Alcohol.**
>
> —Seinfeld

When she came to counseling, Gail was a goal-setting machine. She wanted to run a half marathon. She aimed to graduate in the top 10 percent of her law school class. She was developing coping skills for her seasonal depression. At the bottom of her goal list was her scariest task: *start dating*.

Gail had never planned on delaying her dating life. She was a romantic at heart. She'd had plenty of crushes over the years. But when she looked back over the last decade, she diagnosed herself with a case of As Soon As Syndrome. "I'll date as soon as I get into a good college. As soon as I finish college. As soon as I get into law school." Now she was telling herself, "As soon as I pass the bar." Gail feared that a long line of perfectly legitimate excuses stretched into her busy future as a power spinster.

Gail told me that she felt insecure about not having any experience with sex or romantic relationships. I offered that she didn't have to date if it wasn't something she valued, societal norms be damned. "But it is something I want," she said. "How I spend my time does not always reflect what I really value. Every year it was always easier to just bump it to the bottom of the list."

As a writer whose house becomes squeaky clean whenever I have a deadline, I could certainly relate to Gail. So often our values and our time simply don't match up because we're letting anxiety dictate what we do. And your anxiety will always choose what's safest and most familiar to you. Gail's anxiety was most comfortable with lofty academic goals. Venturing outside of this terrain into the bizarre land of flirtation seemed like a terrible idea. "Why don't we just keep our clothes on and stay in the library," her anxiety suggested. "We love the library!"

Dating is one of the most common topics in my work. In a technology-based, hook-up culture, looking for a mate can be frustrating. There's an incredibly high risk of rejection, and if you didn't have a complex when you started, dating apps will give you one. But whether you're old, young, gay, straight, monogamous, or polyamorous, one thing remains constant—staying focused on being yourself when you're looking for a partner is one of the absolute hardest things to do. We are so quick to sacrifice ourselves for the pleasure of perfect strangers.

Use Your Brain

Gail's anxiety had a lot of valid excuses not to start the process of dating. What if the apps were confusing or overwhelming? What if no one wanted to go out with her? If someone did want to go out with her, how would they react when they found out she'd never been in a relationship? That she'd never had sex? Or even scarier, what if they didn't care and wanted to hook up? How would she even know what to do? As the questions flooded her mind, her anxiety would yell, "ABORT!"

Gail was using certain parts of her brain to solve this problem while ignoring others that could be more useful to her. To investigate this dilemma, we divided her brain (in a drawing obviously) into three parts: a reptilian brain, a mammalian brain, and a human brain.

Reptilian brain: fight, flight, or freeze instincts
Mammalian brain: leaning on relationships
Human brain: working toward a defined goal

Gail's reptilian or "lizard brain" had largely called the shots when it came to her dating life. She'd flee or freeze up when anyone expressed interest in her. But she'd also used that mammalian part of her brain by accessing her relationships to help manage the stress. She fretted to her friends about dating. She listened to success and horror stories about dating in DC. She relied on her friends and parents for encouragement when she couldn't summon the nerve to begin. But nothing seemed to get her there.

By assuming that dating was supposed to be fun and natural, Gail had neglected to access the human part of her brain. Her ability to work toward a defined goal was going to be more useful to her than any pep talk from me or her friends. After all, she was a pro at accomplishing goals—no one needed to teach her. So why not trust her amazing brain when it came to this particular problem?

Dating felt overwhelming. But you know what else is overwhelming? Law school. So how did Gail refrain from being overwhelmed with school? She explained that she managed her school anxiety by only focusing on what was her responsibility for a single day. "I ask myself, 'What do I need to do today to be successful?'" Here was her answer.

Gail began to ask herself what she needed to do first in order to succeed at dating. She decided that before she could take any additional steps, she needed to learn about dating apps to determine which might be a good fit for her. She set the goal of finding one article to read that compared various apps. Suddenly she had tangible, achievable homework, and damn it if this overachiever didn't love homework! The front part of her brain had lit up, illuminating a workable path to dating.

Principles Are Sexy

Gail's confidence grew as she picked a dating app, created a profile, and started messaging with some guys and ignoring the gross ones. Though she was tempted to fudge the truth, she did her best to present her authentic self in her profile. But once her first date rolled around, this self was nowhere to be found. Guy #1 was attractive and impressive, and the entire evening she floated above herself in horror as she agreed with his perfectly inane statements. When he mentioned his disdain for religion, she neglected to mention her involvement with her synagogue. When Guy #1 expressed a desire to move back to Los Angeles, she didn't mention she had a massive cardigan collection and hated applying sunscreen.

After all of her agreeing, it was no surprise that this guy wanted to go out with Gail again. Or he wanted to go out with the pseudo-self her anxiety had so quickly crafted in the face of potential rejection. Gail was 100-percent guy-focused instead of self-focused, making it nearly impossible to hold onto herself.

You might point out that had Gail made a clearer list of what she was looking for in a mate, she might have avoided the trap of self-erasure. People will often make lists of what they're looking for in a significant other and bring them to therapy. I'm happy to hear these thoughts, but I'm way more interested in what people expect out of themselves. Who is the person you want to be on a date? In a relationship? If a potential mate enters from stage right, how does your true self become compromised? Knowing yourself is the best way to ensure that a prospective partner will get to meet them.

There's an anxious way to date, and there's a mature way. Asking yourself the difference between these two paths can give you valuable insight into what to do and what not to do. Remember when we talked about how our anxious autopilot operates in our families? Dating works the same way. You've got to know how you're going to act, so that you can do the opposite.

I asked Gail to imagine that she was pursuing dating in the most anxious way possible and to describe her potential behaviors. Here's what she came up with:

Anxious dating looks like:
- canceling at the last minute
- agreeing with everything a guy says
- saying yes to physical stuff when I'm not ready
- obsessing over messages on apps
- asking for advice from friends without using my own thinking
- avoiding difficult conversations to delay the inevitable
- ghosting someone without being honest

When Gail reversed this list, suddenly she had a list of guiding principles for this new adventure:

Mature dating looks like:
- following through with my plans
- sharing my thinking even when it's different
- saying no when I'm not ready
- setting boundaries on app use
- developing my thinking before I consult others
- pursuing difficult conversations when necessary
- showing respect and honesty when I'm not interested

Now Gail had a road map for how she wanted to function in the dating world. It wasn't her job to get anyone to like her—what a relief. She simply had to stay focused on these principles. Simple, right? Errrr, maybe not. It's easier to stick to your principles when you're a badass singleton. But add another human into the mix, and the game to hold onto yourself truly begins.

Plz Txt Me Back

Gail found that her dating Kryptonite was a common one—her phone. She got better at being honest on dates and trusting her own thinking. But when it came to communicating with guys, her anxiety remained stubbornly at the controls. After a good date, she'd spend the next twenty-four hours absolutely glued to her phone, waiting for a text or app message from a guy to secure the next date.

A person can have every intention of staying calm and collected when a new love interest enters the scene, but technology often keeps us from staying focused on ourselves. Our phones and social media allow us to take a laser-like focus on this new person.

Post-date purgatory looks like:
- excessively Googling someone
- excavating their past social media
- checking to see if they've logged into an app
- texting your friends to analyze the last date
- checking to see if they've seen your text or post

This can be anxiety-producing and mildly infuriating. Someone has time to share a baby goat video on Twitter but not answer your text? All of a sudden it's three a.m., and you're on Facebook dissecting their last trip to Mexico with their ex, wondering if you'll ever be able to make paddle boarding look that sexy (probably not). When you like someone, you can spend a lot of time imagining what a person is thinking, saying, or doing. And if you're not careful, you will begin to treat these imaginings as if they are reality.

This is exactly what happened to Gail. She would go out with someone she really liked, and then she would quickly grow impatient when he didn't text or call right away. If she saw that he had been active on a dating app, she grew furious. Clearly this was ridiculous, as she was also logging in and talking to other people. Unable to get comfortable in post-date purgatory, she found herself blowing up matches and deleting contacts to avoid being ghosted or dumped. She was embarrassed by how near-strangers had such control over her emotions.

Gail convinced herself that she had to slow down and learn to be okay with waiting. No relationship would cement itself in even a week, much less twenty-four hours. So when she started seeing someone she really liked, she limited herself to one nice text afterward, expressing that she had fun and would like to go out again sometime. And then the wait began. She tried everything to distract herself. She went for a run. She called her mom. She read ahead on her assignments. None of it worked that well. She came into therapy begging me for a cure to her anxiety. How could she possibly calm down?

So often with anxiety, our focus is on getting rid of it. This is fine! It's good to practice healthy behaviors that can help manage it. But I'm not certain that you can force yourself to be less reactive in anxiety-producing situations. Tolerance to unfamiliar terrain takes time, as you practice being mature and realizing that you won't die. When you do something risky, like be vulnerable with a stranger who might reject you, anxiety is part of the game. And this is when we are tempted to fall back on those old, automatic habits that get us into trouble.

When a guy didn't immediately text her back, Gail's quickest options for lowering her anxiety would be to:

- send an angry text asking why she hadn't heard from him
- constantly ask friends for reassurance that she'd hear from him
- stop dating all together

These actions were her autopilot, and shutting off her autopilot would certainly make her *more* anxious. But that anxiety would be a sign that she was following her principles: That the adult in her was in control and she was not letting the infant run the show.

Gail wasn't forever destined to be incredibly anxious while she dated. This was simply a temporary increase in anxiety while she learned to navigate dating and waiting to hear back from someone. Living by your principles does get easier, but that takes time. The most she could do was take care of herself, try her best not to focus on the guy, and wait it out.

Redefining Successful Dating

So what happened with Gail and this last guy? Well, he finally got around to texting her. They kept seeing each other, and he kept up his magic act of disappearing and reappearing. After a few dates, Gail shared with him that it was confusing to not hear from him for long stretches of time. She said that a relationship was something she was looking for, and that if he wasn't interested in at least thinking about that, then they'd have to part ways. And part ways they did. He's probably out still roaming Capitol Hill bars infuriating women with his aloofness.

By the world's definition, this series of interactions would be deemed a failure. Gail hadn't convinced a guy to stop being shifty and see how great she was. But that wasn't Gail's responsibility. My guess was that she'd dodged months of frustration by getting to the point sooner rather than later. So often we're afraid we'll scare someone off by sharing what we want and what we won't put up with. But as someone who's watched marriages end when people are finally forced to have these conversations, I'd call this outcome a huge success.

One idea in Bowen theory is that people tend to end up with other people who are at the same level of differentiation, or emotional maturity, as they are. So if you consider that you'll go on dates with people of varying levels of maturity, it makes sense that a lot of these dates won't end successfully. This can help you feel less rejected and more objective.

When you begin to define successful dating as sticking with your principles, then you've turned the focus back on yourself and can usually calm down. This doesn't mean you'll necessarily have great success right away, but it does mean that you're likely to end up with someone at that same level of maturity. Sexy, right?

Your Questions

Observe

- What does dating anxiously look like for me?
- When have I become too other-focused after a date?
- When have I been quick to obscure my true self from a love interest?

Evaluate

- How would I define dating maturely for me?
- What beliefs or values do I need to communicate more clearly with a love interest?
- What wisdom would I like to remember when I'm tempted to obsess over a love interest?

Interrupt

- How can I practice being more self-focused when I'm dating?
- How can I shut off my anxious autopilot when I'm dating?
- Are there tools or people who can help me be my best self when I'm dating?

Your Practice

Whether we're dating or not, we're all more than willing to chip away at ourselves to get people to like us. Do you hold an uncommon political or religious belief in your peer group? Are you hesitant to admit you have an encyclopedic knowledge of the *Real Housewives* franchise? Take a few minutes to make a quick list of every belief, interest, value, or trait that you've hidden or lied about to attain the love or approval of another person. Take a look at the list, and consider how you can do a better job of defining yourself to a new love interest and to existing relationships.

CHAPTER 8

Love

Is not general incivility the very essence of love?
—*Elizabeth in Jane Austen's Pride and Prejudice*

Marcus and Sarah were close. I mean literally close—they lived in a four-hundred-square-foot apartment. Marcus was a thirty-five-year-old restaurant manager who came to counseling because he was certain he'd have a heart attack before he hit forty. He told me that his physical health often took a backseat to work problems and relationship drama. Marcus was continually stressed out by high turnover at the restaurant. And he complained that his girlfriend of three years wasn't supportive of his career goals or his health goals. She wanted to get married, and he wasn't sure if he wanted to commit.

Marcus and Sarah had met on a friend's ultimate Frisbee team and immediately hit it off. After a few months, Sarah moved into his apartment. Three years later, they still spent most of their time with each other. They commuted together. They ate lunch together. They were constantly checking in via text when they were apart. To an outsider, they seemed like two peas in a small pod.

Well past the honeymoon stage, Marcus still found that he would grow increasingly anxious when Sarah wasn't around. He became paranoid when she went to happy hours with her male friends from work. In turn, Sarah would complain when he spent time with his college roommates without her. They'd fight about it, and then she'd log into his iPad to see if he was complaining to friends about her.

Because of this intense togetherness, Marcus and Sarah began to aggravate each other. Sarah would snap at Marcus when he worked long hours and let his share of the chores slip, or she'd give him the cold shoulder as she angrily banged dishes in the kitchen. Marcus accused Sarah of sabotaging his diet attempts, as she would buy tons of junk food and bring it home. "I can't meet my goals with Doritos in the house!" he'd snap at her. After these arguments, they'd go to their friends and their therapists to complain about the other until they calmed down. Then it was back to constant contact once again.

Get Off the Blame Train

People often come to counseling very focused on their partner. In that first session, they will catalog their partner's faults like a prosecutor giving his closing statement. Because anxiety makes us other-focused, we're skilled at knowing our partner's many flaws. You can remember the times they forgot to take out the garbage or text you when they were running late, but that time you watched a *Game of Thrones* episode without them gets shoved way back into brain storage. Because examples of your partner's flaws are so readily available, they make great evidence when your brain is trying to piece together who's at fault.

Marcus found it easy to blame Sarah for his unhealthy habits. Despite her love of junk food, Sarah was in better shape, and it made him feel insecure. She spent a lot of time exercising at the gym where she worked, and he often instigated arguments when he felt guilty about not functioning "on her level." Sarah would go for early morning runs, while Marcus, exhausted from a long night at the restaurant, would stay in bed and mentally beat himself up.

How did Marcus choose to manage his anxiety about his health? He asked Sarah to stop inviting him to exercise: "It makes me feel like you're judging me when I say no." He asked her to stop buying the foods she wanted and to stop sprinkling cheese on her salads: "If we're going to be healthy, then we need to mean it!"

So often we demand others change as a way of managing our own insecurities. This reflects the other-focus of anxiety—"If you would just stop doing X, then I would be okay." We look to others to fill in the gaps of our own emotional maturity, to overfunction while we underfunction. It can be useful to take this blaming and flip it back as a challenge to yourself—not to blame but to begin to claim responsibility for your own anxiety. I call it the "Blaming to Claiming" exercise.

Let's Practice!

Blaming: I would have applied for that job if you were more encouraging, Chandra!

Claiming: I am responsible for my career decisions.

Blaming: I'd have been on time if you hadn't taken ten years to eat that bagel, Steve!

Claiming: I am in charge of when I arrive at work.

Blaming: It's impossible for me to meditate when you're marathoning *The Great British Baking Show*!

Claiming: I can leave the room or wear headphones when I need to focus.

Now this doesn't mean that you can't ever talk about your partner's behavior or that you can't be legitimately wronged by someone. This is about when the lines of responsibility blur and we are quick to put others in charge of our destiny and functioning. Because the truth is, being less responsible for your partner and more responsible for yourself usually calms things down. And when things are calmer, intimacy can more naturally occur. You also usually level up on your overall functioning.

Are You Separate People or a Relationship Blob?

When you live with your partner, it becomes easy to treat them like an extension of yourself rather than an independent human being. Emotions and responsibilities tend to blur. It's easy to get caught in the dynamic of over/underfunctioning. You may find that it's impossible for you to remain calm if your partner is anxious, and vice versa. Because of this, your focus shifts to calming them down rather than calming yourself. This is exactly what happened with Sarah and Marcus. They struggled to remain differentiated, separate people, morphing together as one anxious blob of a relationship. We called it the SARCUS, a portmanteau of their names.

Sarah struggled to hold down a full-time job. She worked a few hours a week as a spin instructor, but Marcus paid most of the rent and bills. Marcus believed that if he pushed Sarah too hard to find a job, it would trigger a huge fight. Exhausted from work, he simply didn't have the energy to deal with this pushback. It was easier to just pay the bills to keep things temporarily calm than to cause an increase in anxiety and risk the relationship.

Similarly, Sarah feared Marcus's sensitivity about his health. She began to sneak out of the apartment in the mornings so her exercising wouldn't upset him. She hid her junk food in her car or scarfed it down before she got home, so he wouldn't yell at her for sabotaging his diet. They were both tiptoeing around the other's sensitivities, not wanting to wake the SARCUS.

As an outsider, it's easy to look at Marcus and say, "Dude, just stop paying for her stuff!" Or tell Sarah, "Eat what you want and let him deal with it!" But it's not that easy to separate a relationship blob into two people.

When Marcus began the work of untangling their intense togetherness, I asked him, "How would you like to be less responsible for Sarah?" He came up with this list:

- I'd like to tell her that I can no longer pay her phone bill.
- I'd like to let her manage her own emotions when I hang out with my friends.
- I'd like to not respond to her texts right away if I'm busy at work.

These were tangible tasks that Marcus could track. They were certain to make Sarah a little distressed, but over time they would claim back some energy that Marcus could put toward his own goals. "How would you like to use this freed-up energy to be more responsible for yourself?" I asked him.

- I'd like to take a few minutes at work to de-stress so I'm not shoving food in my face.
- I'd like to manage my own emotions when Sarah eats junk food.
- I'd like to wake up fifteen minutes earlier so I can walk to work.

By focusing less on functioning for Sarah and more on his own responsibilities, Marcus was learning to be more of a self. He was beginning to distinguish between being a supportive partner and managing Sarah to keep things calm. If she had a problem at work, he listened instead of trying to fix it. If she complained about her credit card bill, he didn't offer to pay it. Over time, Marcus began to notice that when he was more focused on his physical and mental health, Sarah began to focus more on her own responsibilities. The SARCUS was losing its power, and two capable individuals were emerging.

Caught in a Cycle

As Marcus began to work on himself and let Sarah do the same, he found himself thinking more about the future. Sarah didn't figure prominently in these imaginings, but he was terrified to ask her if she felt the same way. Marcus admitted that many evenings when he and Sarah were at home together, they would smoke pot or drink to ease the tension. Slipping back into blaming mode, Marcus complained that she poured too much into his glass when they drank. These substances would calm things down, but ultimately resentments would build up again. They'd explode into a fight, retreat to complain to friends, and then make up when they calmed down. But each time, they were too anxious to bring up their true relationship concerns.

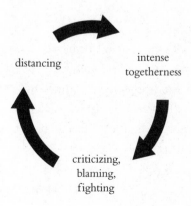

They were worried that a real conversation would end the relationship. They were caught in a cycle of closeness, conflict, and distance that spun around and around.

People can get stuck in this kind of cycle for years. Intense togetherness in the relationship blob makes you allergic to the other person. The slightest annoyance can lead to an explosive fight, or contact with others can trigger paranoia about cheating. To manage their anxiety, people often turn to other people to calm down, creating triangles. A triangle could involve having an affair, complaining to a friend, or even talking to a therapist. Once these outsiders help manage the anxiety, both are calm enough to return to the intense togetherness that began the cycle.

It's important to note that intense togetherness does not equal intimacy. Marcus and Sarah had tricked themselves into thinking that living together and being in constant contact equaled a solid relationship. But it didn't. They were chatting constantly, but they weren't communicating. They were using activities, alcohol, and other people to manage their anxiety. These strategies were keeping their relationship on life support, and neither was willing to finally let go.

What Is Love?

So if the goal is for two people to function as capable individuals, what about romance? Is the "ridiculous, inconvenient, consuming, can't-live-without-each-other love" claimed by Carrie Bradshaw just a lie? Well, kind of. People live without each other all the time. Our partners walk the dog without us. They go on work trips. Sometimes they break up with us, or even die, and yet we live. Sure, it's cute when two married ninety-seven-year-olds die within twenty-four hours of each other. But most of us want to love and also be resilient as hell.

Humans are relationship creatures. We're not meant to exist in the world alone. We do really need each other to build homes or make babies or feel secure. And that's great! But we're also individuals. We climb mountains and write novels and cure diseases. We have goals and interests that are just about us. Less anxious love is a balance between these two great forces—individuality and togetherness. Partners must work and play together but also respect the individual in each other. If they can't, they end up being two people who are just trying to calm each other down all day long.

Marcus and Sarah were so focused on maintaining calmness in the relationship that they had delayed sharing what they wanted as individuals. But by working on being more of a self in the relationship, Marcus slowly progressed toward having the big conversation. He asked Sarah to sit down one evening, declined his usual mega-glass of wine, and shared that he wanted a partner who contributed financially to the household. He told Sarah that he wasn't interested in staying in DC. He wanted to start his own restaurant, and right now he wasn't interested in having children.

You can guess what happened. Marcus and Sarah realized that each of them had different expectations for the future and for marriage. They realized that though they loved each other, neither was the partner they wanted for the long term. After a few heartbreaking conversations, they broke up, and Marcus moved out of their tiny space.

I'm sharing this story with you because I call it a success, not a failure. Building a stronger sense of self in a relationship does not mean that the relationship will succeed. But it does give you a greater chance of finding one with less anxiety, a relationship with the right balance of individuality and togetherness. We need each other, but boy do we need ourselves.

Your Questions

Observe

- When do I blame my partner instead of claiming responsibility for myself?
- How do I let my partner function for me when I'm anxious?
- When do I triangle in other people rather than talking directly to my partner?

Evaluate

- What would being more responsible for myself in my relationship look like?
- What would being less responsible for my partner look like?
- What wisdom would I like to remember so I can be my best self in a relationship?

Interrupt

- How can I interrupt automatic behaviors (like underfunctioning and triangling) in my relationship?
- What can I do this week to take responsibility for my anxiety in my relationship?
- What are upcoming opportunities when I can practice being more of an individual in my relationship?

Your Practice

When someone loves us, they want to be helpful to us. So it can be easy for us to begin to underfunction and let the relationship blob take over. Especially when we're stressed! Take a few minutes and make a list of all the times in a relationship it's been easier to just let your partner do something for you. What abilities grew rusty over time? What did you never learn to do? Would you like to be able to change a tire, make an omelet, or calm yourself down? Make a second list of all the skills you'd like to learn or relearn so that you can be a capable, separate person in your relationship. There's nothing sexier!

CHAPTER 9

Making Friends

> **It is more fun to talk with someone who doesn't use long, difficult words but rather short, easy words like "What about lunch?"**
>
> —Winnie-the-Pooh

Mira came to counseling because she was exhausted and lonely. She was a first-year PhD student studying history, and she had arrived in DC anticipating a rich social life. Freshly graduated from a rural college, the twenty-three-year-old had imagined late nights full of intellectual banter in quirky bars with fascinating city-dwellers. But Mira's anxiety had other plans for her, and her high hopes of a new fancy life were swallowed up by reality. She felt foolish that she had expected fiercely loyal friends to land in her lap like in her favorite TV shows.

It certainly didn't help that Mira's grad school classmates were a competitive and anxious bunch. They were all keenly aware that someday they'd be competing for a handful of academic jobs. And when they did hang out, they whined about their professors and their workload. She came home every day feeling despondent and found no safe haven. Her four intimidating housemates seemed like typical Washingtonians—they worked, exercised, and drank like professionals. Everywhere she turned, Mira felt as if she weren't smart enough to trick anybody into hanging out with her.

So naturally, Mira began to take the advice that her anxiety gave her: *abort socializing!* She hibernated in her room that winter. Class readings took a backseat to rewatching her favorite shows in bed. This procrastination further fueled her doubts that she was worthy of a spot in her academic program. She also grew more skittish around her roommates. Rather than put her poor cooking skills on display in their shared kitchen, Mira blew through her bank account with nightly takeout. She slept in on the weekends and stopped returning calls from old friends. Mira was depressed, and grad school was officially the worst.

When she came to counseling, Mira knew that what she needed most was simple—other humans. She suspected there was no way she'd finish grad school in a carefully constructed bubble. She craved the synchronous living that she had experienced with her college roommates. A small student body and rural setting had driven them together like magnets. Now she faced the challenge of learning to make friends as an adult, which brought all of her insecurities front and center.

Anxiety and Friendships

Relationships have a lot to do with our mood, our health, and our behaviors, and a solid network of friends can lower your risk of illness, divorce, and even death. Interacting with friends gives you a kick of endorphins, which boost your immune system and lower anxiety, and oxytocin, an important bonding hormone that can help with depression. Women in particular seem to need these connections more than men. Researchers have found that women receive these benefits when they see their friends at least twice a week.

We miss out on fizzy endorphins and fuzzy oxytocin when we

let anxiety dictate who we are and how we operate with friends or potential friends. Anxiety is a diluting agent in human relationships. In its effort to keep things calm and under our control, it turns our friendships into watered-down versions of the real thing.

Mira's anxiety was definitely calling the shots in her life. She assumed that everyone she encountered was more accomplished or more fabulous than her awkward self. Her anxiety propelled her brain straight back to her high school days, when the boundaries between social hierarchies were impenetrable. By obscuring reality and imposing this fear, her anxiety made building friendships seem impossible.

Lucky for us, we are smarter and more creative than our anxiety. Remember those four predictable strategies we discussed in Chapter 5? They aren't just at work in our families—we use them in our existing and potential friendships. And when you can observe them, you can absolutely interrupt them.

Mira began to observe her functioning with prospective friends, and she found that she was an expert at using triangles and distance to keep things calm.

Triangles

Shaky friendships are often stabilized by triangles. When a conversation grows boring, maybe you start to gossip about another friend's love life. Perhaps a friendship is built on your mutual disdain for classmates, a coworker, or even an actor. If you're skeptical, grab a friend, and see how long you both can talk about each other before you shift to talking about a third person. Difficult, right?

Mira could see how her friendships with her fellow PhD students were like a two-legged stool—without a third person to bitch about, they weren't steady. Her school friendships were built on their mutual disdain for their professors. Lunch conversations poked fun at those who gave terrible lectures or had questionable fashion sense. When they ran out of funny anecdotes, they vented about their workload or dismal employment prospects. Though she enjoyed griping in the moment, Mira always left these gatherings feeling irritable. She didn't know the first thing about her classmates, and she imagined that they weren't particularly interested in getting to know her. She looked at them and saw people wealthier and smarter than she was. Maybe the chaos and resentments of grad school were the only elements that could sustain their camaraderie. It wasn't a friendship—it was a ventship.

Distance

Distance is a common strategy for managing anxiety in friendships or potential ones. Maybe you can only meet new people if you've had a drink. Perhaps you play it safe at social gatherings, only talking about the weather or work. If you're truly passionate about meteorology, then knock yourself out. Otherwise, consider that you may be holding back your true interests, passions, and thoughts out of a fear of rejection or disapproval.

There is no end to the way we duck, dodge, and bat away being truly seen by others. Maybe you use sarcasm or block compliments like a World Cup goalie. When we distance, our pseudo-selves are hard at work, making it seem as if we're cooler or less cool than we really are. All this work at distancing turns us into bland, dispassionate people. You can make a lot of acquaintances by playing it safe, but few true friends.

Mira was a master at using distance with potential friends. Sure, there was the physical distance created by hiding in her room or skipping social events. But she was emotionally distancing by refusing to share what was really on her mind or what really excited her. She let her acquaintances dictate the conversation, even if it bored her to tears. When she did offer up a shaky opinion, she apologized for the audacity of having a thought.

Mira also used distance by refusing help from people who cared about her. When she got food poisoning, she couldn't even ask someone to accompany her to the emergency room. Yet without blinking, she was the first to reach for a restaurant bill she couldn't afford or offer to feed the pet of a virtual stranger for a month. She was happy to cross the boundary between friend and pushover but defended the walls between herself and others with vigilance.

Over time, the gulf between her safe self and her real self grew wider. It felt impossible to bridge.

HOW WE MANAGE ANXIETY IN FRIENDSHIPS

Triangles	Over/ Underfunctioning	Conflict	Distance
• gossiping • venting • scapegoating • criticizing • blaming others • needing a buffer to hang out	• always being in charge • giving advice • constantly reassuring • always letting others decide • relying on reassurance • acting helpless	• thriving on drama • focusing on flaws • seeing others as the problem • insisting that others change	• sticking to superficial topics • using sarcasm • drinking or getting high • dismissing compliments • bailing at the last minute

The Terror of Vulnerability

Anxiety-managing behaviors can suck up all our friendship energy. There's little left to be ourselves and just freaking relax. It feels impossible to be vulnerable in a friendship based on gossiping or sarcasm, or in one that might erupt into conflict at any time.

So far we've talked a lot about functioning as a self, or an individual. But being more responsible for yourself doesn't mean you live like a hermit. It doesn't mean that you never ask for help. In fact, it strengthens your ability to be vulnerable in your friendships. It gives you the courage to lean on people when you need to do so. The more differentiated person can share their thinking, beliefs, and interests even if a friend disagrees with them or doesn't understand them.

What is vulnerability? Dr. Brené Brown (aka Vulnerability Guru) defines the term as "uncertainty, risk, and emotional exposure." Anxiety keeps us from taking this risk in our friendships. Anxiety wants us to maintain the status quo. So if you've always talked about football with your friends, your anxiety absolutely does not think you should bring up your parents' divorce. If you're the high school friend who always plans reunions, your anxiety won't let you take a break and allow someone else to do the heavy lifting. If you're the only conservative in your friend group, your anxiety wants you to shut up when your liberal friends are riffing on political news.

As I've said before, the question is never whether these strategies are unhealthy or healthy. A better question is this: What is the cost? What do you miss out on when you listen to your anxiety in your friendships? Maybe it's a closer connection with an acquaintance. Perhaps it's the ability to receive help when you need it. Maybe you drag out a friendship that should have ended a long time ago. When you ask this question, you might find that the terror of vulnerability is 100 percent worth it.

Taking Up Space

After she spent some time observing her insecurities, Mira found that she was ready to scare herself with some vulnerability. She was tired of refusing to let her true self exist in the world. Her anxiety wanted her to erase any part of herself that might cause awkwardness or disapproval. What remained was the shell of a person who would mold to the opinions or behaviors of others or recede into the background. No wonder she was depressed.

"I just want to take up some space!" she said.

Together we considered what it would look like for Mira to take up space in her friendships. Here are the ideas she generated.

Mira's Friendship Principles

- I will be honest when I'm having a hard day, and let people react however they want.
- I will ask for help and accept help when I need it.
- I will tell new friends I like them and want to spend time with them.
- I will talk about what genuinely excites me.
- I will move around as if I belong in the world.

Armed with some solid principles, Mira was reducing the odds that her anxious autopilot would kick in. She suddenly had other options than just triangling or distancing. She could feel insecure, but she didn't have to *act* insecure.

Mira decided that the easiest place to start was with her classmates. She wanted to develop real relationships with these people—they shared common interests and would be stuck together for at least five years. It didn't take long for an opportunity to present itself. They were grabbing dinner after class one day, and the conversation quickly devolved into complaining about a particular professor. Here was her moment! Mira took a deep breath, turned to the guy next to her, and said, "I want to tell you about this novel I'm reading. I think you might like it." To her surprise, he was thrilled with the change of subject.

Encouraged by her success at school, Mira decided to start taking up some space at home. It was time to tackle her fear of cooking in front of other people. One Saturday afternoon, she bought ingredients to make a pie, and she literally took up some space in the kitchen. Inevitably, one of her roommates walked by in the middle of her disastrous pie making. In the past, Mira would have abandoned her efforts all together or apologized for making a mess in the kitchen. So now it was her job to do the opposite of what her anxiety would have her do. Heart racing, she turned to her housemate and exclaimed, "I have no idea what I'm doing! But you're welcome to help if you'd like." An hour later she had one mediocre apple pie and a budding friendship.

Over the spring semester, Mira became a three-dimensional human again as she began to take up space. She called old friends when she felt lonely, even if she was worried she might be bothering them. She didn't start phone conversations with the phrase, "Is this a bad time?" She trusted that it was the responsibility of others to tell her if she was inconveniencing them or to change the subject if she was boring them.

By working on her level of differentiation in her friendships, Mira was finding the space between isolation and complete dependence. She could take risks and survive rejection. The world didn't end when people didn't text her back or didn't seem interested in getting to know her. She focused her energy on the people who did, and she learned not to be shy about telling people she wanted to be their friends. It was unusually bold, and she almost always got a positive response. After all, who doesn't like being told that they're interesting and worth knowing? People love that.

Mira also began to realize that the mature relationships she was building were more valuable than the fictional "ride or die" friendships she had once coveted. She had longed for a friend who would call her at three a.m. to talk through a non-crisis, but now she enjoyed that her friends were capable humans. She needed friends who loved her and respected her for who she was—not friends who would feel responsible for her anxiety.

More differentiated people tend to have deeper friendships and a greater number of them. They can have friends with different beliefs or experiences from their own. They can be a resource to their friends without feeling responsible for everyone. They can gain friends and lose friends, outgrow friendships and grow into them. This may not make great television, but mature friendships are less exhausting and more interesting. The more you focus on being the person you want to be, the more you will invite people into your life who allow you to be that person.

Your Questions

Observe

- What anxious behaviors keep me from building more fulfilling friendships?
- How do I use my pseudo-self when making friends?
- When is it difficult to be vulnerable with friends?

Evaluate

- What friendship opportunities have I missed because of anxiety?
- What principles would I like to remember when finding friends?
- What aspects of myself would I like to share more in my friendships?

Interrupt

- What upcoming opportunities are there for me to work on friendship insecurities?
- How can I build stronger one-to-one friendships that are less reliant on gossip or venting?

- How can I remember my principles when I feel anxious meeting someone new?

Your Practice

We all have ways that we can bring more self to our friendships. Maybe this means being more honest about a challenge. Perhaps you'd like to talk more about your passions, even if it bores the hell out of people. Maybe you are done feeding someone's demon cat and need to tell them to hire a pet sitter. Pick one friendship in which your anxiety is high, and brainstorm all the ways you'd like to take up space rather than hiding your true thoughts and passions. Taking up space is not about being selfish or mean. It's simply honoring the parts of yourself that aren't up for debate or negotiation.

CHAPTER 10

Finding Community

> The essential dilemma of my life is my deep desire
> to belong and my suspicion of belonging.
>
> —*Jhumpa Lahiri*

Philip came to counseling for a poetic kick in the butt. He was a twenty-six-year-old administrative assistant whose life was in a holding pattern. He had moved to the city to escape his small hometown in Michigan. Two years later, he had few friends outside of work. He had little energy to do anything except watch his dog sniff the takeout containers that littered his apartment. At night he battled insomnia, wondering if he should just call the game and move home.

Philip explained to me that he felt paralyzed when it came to his future. He had done everything he was supposed to do—go to college, save some money, and launch from his parents' house toward a new job and city. But rents were out of control, the government wanted his student loan payments, and a giant void swallowed every job application he sent. Philip was stuck, and his anxiety was blasting on full volume.

When we get laser-focused on something we really want, we forget that there is more than one way to grow. I asked Philip what he wanted to do to build up a stronger sense of self while he waited for his career to unfold. Philip told me that what he really wanted was to join a poetry group. He had minored in creative writing in college with a focus on poetry.

Philip admitted he felt anxious about launching himself into a new group of strangers. Would they not take him seriously, since he hadn't written in years? Would it just be a hodgepodge of weirdos with too much free time? The whole idea felt like more trouble than it was worth.

Stop Making Excuses

Anxiety is a condition best fueled by isolation and rumination. When we deny ourselves community, we lose contact with thoughtful and passionate people who will challenge our worst beliefs about ourselves. But we often treat community like a luxury rather than an essential component of our well-being.

Often this avoidance of community is your anxiety wearing the mask of self-denial. Because your anxiety loves to find reasons to keep you away from community, it will offer you unwatched TV seasons and pizza in bed. It will remind you that you have nothing to wear or that there's a 20 percent chance of rain. It will pull out your to-do lists, point to your laundry pile, and suggest it's simply not a good time to throw yourself into unfamiliar terrain. It's easy to develop As Soon As Syndrome when it comes to exploring new community. Have you ever used an As Soon As excuse to deny yourself community?

- I'll join a Frisbee team as soon as I get settled at work.
- I'll start going back to religious services as soon as the semester is over.
- I'll check out that running group as soon as I can finish a 5K by myself.
- I'm going to move next year, so I'll start volunteering as soon as I get settled.

When we treat community as if it's something to be earned, we forget that community is where we learn to define ourselves to others, to be the person we want to be. Without community, it's unlikely you'll ever feel settled or calm down. Community is the cake, not the icing. But our anxiety will often tell us otherwise.

Philip and I talked about the As Soon As excuses he used to hold back from community. He had been telling himself that he'd join a writing group as soon as he had a new job, visible abs, and a journal full of new poetry. When he said these excuses out loud, he realized that he'd set the bar far too high. He could sit at home and stew about his unaccomplished goals, or he could live his life and have some cake. He scoured the Internet and soon had a list of three potential poetry meet-ups. But he didn't arrive at the meet-ups alone—he brought his anxiety with him.

Community Is Imperfect

It takes a lot of courage to insert yourself into a group of strangers. But showing up is just the beginning. When you arrive, you're likely to find that a community is full of these anxious creatures known as humans. People in a group will have varying levels of maturity and anxiety. And like our families, any group is likely to use those anxiety-managing strategies we've discussed. Conflict is inevitable. Triangles will emerge when people are unhappy with a group member or leader. People will distance themselves and cut off when they're not happy with a decision. Some members will try to control everything, and others will not carry their weight.

Philip described the poetry meet-ups he'd visited, and it sounded like a literary *Goldilocks and the Three Bears*. The first meeting was too chaotic, he said. People bristled too much while their poems were being critiqued, and no one seemed to be in charge of planning. The second meeting was too intimidating—many people in the group had

MFAs and bragged about getting published. He left the first group feeling exhausted and the second feeling insecure.

Philip never found out if the third group was just right because he was too discouraged to try it out. His pride had already been wounded from a discouraging job search, and he hadn't anticipated how reactive he'd feel among people giving each other feedback. His anxiety was looking for reasons to bail, and it found a buffet of excuses at these poetry groups.

When you enter into a new community, it can be useful to prepare yourself for your anxiety's response. After all, your anxiety's job is to sniff out potential threats and snubs in a new environment. But your job is to dial down the melodrama and stick with the reality-based, principled thinking that can help you decide whether a group is right for you.

Let's Practice!

Scenario: You attend a religious service, and no one approaches you to say hello.

Anxious Thinking: How dare no one appreciate me! I am a delight!

Principled Thinking: Introducing myself to people I'd like to know is my responsibility.

Scenario: You visit a local political group and find the meeting slightly disorganized.

Anxious Thinking: *Must take control to save the republic.*

Principled Thinking: Not everyone will be as efficient as I am, and that's okay!

Scenario: You join a softball team, and they put you in left field.

Anxious Thinking: Time to climb a tree and never leave!

Principled Thinking: I'm here to have fun, not to go pro.

You don't have to force yourself to join a group you hate or to stay in one you've outgrown. But you have to manage your anxiety first, before you can make that decision.

Know Thyself

Joining a group isn't as scary when you can predict how you're going to react. How do you do that? Easy—just look at how you act in your family. If you're the oldest child in your family and like to boss everyone around, you might take on too much responsibility in a group. If you're distant with your parents, you might break off from a community when times get tense or boring. If your family is full of triangles, then you might love to spill the tea. To know thyself is to give yourself a decent shot at doing something different.

Philip was the oldest in his family. He craved order and didn't like being told what to do. If he couldn't be in charge of planning a family dinner, he simply didn't show up. He struggled to watch people be inefficient, but when people proved capable, he felt threatened. So it was not a shock that he felt impatient or under attack when he visited these writing groups. On a good day, perhaps he could bite his lip and be his best self. But this year had been hard, and his automatic functioning was difficult to override. He was focused on everyone else instead of himself. The only way he knew how to manage his reactivity was simply to avoid community altogether.

People often comment that a congregation, a club, or a team is the family they never had. But let's be honest—changing groups does not change how you function. We don't magically become less anxious, more mature people because we're not related to the people around us. We're too hardwired to interrupt our anxious functioning with a simple change of company. At some level of stress, our autopilot will always kick in. It just might take longer with your a capella group than at Grandma's.

Remember how we interrupt our autopilot? We define our principles! Just as it's useful to have guiding principles for how you operate in your family, you should have some ideas about how you want to conduct yourself in any group of humans. Here are some examples.

Principles for Community
- I will find a community whose mission I believe in and endorse.
- I will stay focused on this mission, even in times of anxiety.
- I will define my commitment to this community and honor it.
- I will remember that relationship challenges in community are inevitable.
- I will attempt to manage my own anxious functioning instead of others'.

This might sound completely over the top to you. After all, isn't it unlikely that world events or a delicious scandal is going to shake the very foundation of your gardening club? Perhaps, but anywhere humans are gathered, there will be times of tension. When you have principles to guide you through them, you'll be more prepared to weather the drama or the occasional chaos or arrogance.

Dumbledore's Army

Philip was no Emily Dickinson—he knew that he needed a community to build up his sense of self. But first he had to reframe how he thought about his relationships in a group. He was using the strategies of conflict and distance to manage his anxiety in this community. There was likely to be at least one person more talented than he was, which always set him on the defensive (conflict). And if he saw people as less talented or unorganized, then he felt like quitting (distance). He resented getting feedback either way, and the community became anything but calming. He needed a way to stay connected to the group but exist outside of these emotions. In other words, he needed to work on being more differentiated.

I suggested to Philip that he think of his poetry group as a sort of Dumbledore's Army. In *Harry Potter and the Order of the Phoenix*, Hermione and others assembled a group so that the students of Hogwarts could learn what it was like to face Voldemort. They weren't competing against each other—they were sharing the skills they'd picked up to face a common enemy. It didn't matter who was more advanced and who was just getting started.

Philip was a *Harry Potter* fan who liked this analogy, so he tried imagining his poetry group as an assembled team of people who could support and teach each other on their creative journeys. Their enemy was procrastination or self-doubt or whatever they needed it to be—just not each other. He was taking the problem out of the relationships and putting the challenge back on himself. Philip realized that he didn't need to find a writing community that always praised him or one that ran like a nuclear submarine. He just needed the support of humans who also desired to live a creative life.

After some deliberation, Philip decided to attend the poetry group that challenged him a bit more, even if he felt insecure from time to time. It would take some practice to learn to manage his reactivity, but he could get there if he stuck by his principles. The group could help him learn that criticism was no big deal, which in turn would make his job search feel less hopeless. He knew that he'd land something eventually, and in the meantime he could enjoy life and verse.

Community, like family, is another place where we are challenged to be our best selves. After all, if you can't be yourself while connected to others, can you really be your best self? That is the work of differentiation. Anxiety will come and go, but who we are among others is what truly defines us.

Your Questions

Observe

- How has anxiety kept me from joining a community?
- How does anxiety or insecurity affect my behavior in a community?
- Have I ever regretted cutting off quickly from a group? Why?

Evaluate

- What questions would it be useful to ask myself before joining a group?
- How might I replicate my family dynamics in a community I join?
- What are my principles for calm, mature functioning in a community?

Interrupt

- What groups would I like to join in the next year?
- How can I work on being more comfortable with imperfection in one of my communities?
- How can I access my best thinking in a community when tension is high?

Your Practice

Have you ever suffered from As Soon As Syndrome when you thought about joining a new group or community? How did your anxiety keep you from meeting new people? Did it scold you for not focusing as much on your career or your health? Did it remind you of all the times that other communities disappointed you or rejected you? Take a few minutes to jot down all of the excuses you've used to deny yourself community. Then consider the ways that being in a community can have a positive impact on your life. What group of anxious humans could make life much more interesting?

Let's Review Part 2!

This section was all about navigating anxiety in your relationships. Here's what we learned.

1. **Understand that your family is an anxiety-managing machine.** We benefit when we see ourselves as part of a larger relationship system that is built to manage tension. By looking at the bigger system, we are less likely to blame others and more likely to see the part we play in responding to anxiety.
2. **Know the strategies that groups use to keep things calm.** Our families and other groups use predictable strategies to manage anxiety that can include distance, conflict, over/underfunctioning, and triangles. Everyone plays a part in this emotional process, which is often a multigenerational pattern.
3. **Predict how you will use these strategies when you feel anxious or insecure.** By knowing which anxiety-managing strategies we are likely to use in our relationships, we have a greater chance of interrupting our automatic functioning. We can be more objective and respond to challenges with greater maturity and calmness.
4. **Work on primary relationships to benefit all anxious areas of life.** Contact with our parents and other family members provides an opportunity to work on differentiation and managing our reactiveness. It is difficult to define yourself in these relationships, but the ability to do so can lower anxiety in other areas of life.

5. **Keep defining your principles to navigate tension with others.** To provide an alternative to anxious functioning, you must take the time to define how you would like to respond when you feel insecure or threatened. It can be useful to define principles for navigating challenges like dating, making friends, or operating in a community.

6. **Practice being yourself in relationship to others.** Once you have defined your principles, you must look for opportunities to live them out in times of stress or uncertainty. This often takes many attempts and many failures. But any amount of progress can be life-changing.

If all of these points seem overwhelming, just stay focused on those three verbs—**observe**, **evaluate**, and **interrupt**. Understand how you act when you're anxious. Consider who you'd like to be instead. Then try it out, in all your bumbling glory!

Part Three

✳   ✳   ✳

YOUR ANXIOUS
CAREER

CHAPTER 11

The Job Hunt

Always remember that you are absolutely unique.
Just like everyone else.

—Margaret Mead

Chris never told his parents that he had finished grad school. They would ask him why he was bartending with a master's in museum education. But there he was, ten months after graduation, pouring drinks for tourists instead of knowledge into the heads of children. He had been a little nervous leaving school without a job, but he'd reassured himself that plenty of his classmates were in the same boat. By the time he came to therapy, his brain was fresh out of reassurance. His anxiety told him that his education had been a grand waste of time.

Looking for a job is a particularly anxious endeavor. Take the insecurity of being unemployed or underemployed, turn up the pressure with a shrinking bank account, add expectations from family and society, and you've cooked yourself one piping hot dish of panic casserole. It doesn't help that most job searches are impersonal and perplexing—submitting an application online feels more like sending a message in a bottle than communicating with another human.

All of these factors left Chris feeling reactive and fatigued. He described how he'd taken a night gig bartending so he'd have free time during the day to apply to jobs. Most nights he would set his alarm for seven a.m. so he could head to a coffee shop and work. But when morning rolled around, he'd hit snooze a dozen times. By midmorning, his overwhelming guilt had dulled any motivation to get started.

Embarrassed by his procrastination, Chris kept lying to his family about still being in school. He stopped hanging out with friends who gave him sympathetic frowns, and he avoided social situations in which people asked the inevitable question, "What do you do?" This isolation fueled his self-criticism, which further cemented him to the bed each morning. He had no idea how to break the cycle.

Attacking and Avoiding

In his quest to find a museum job, Chris seesawed back and forth between attacking the problem and avoiding it all together. He came home at two a.m. from the bar, exhausted and cranky. But his anxiety kept him awake, and he spent hours in the dark scrolling through job sites. He worked himself into a frenzy and would submit his résumé for bizarre museum jobs in nowheresville that he didn't even want. If a job seemed interesting but required more work to apply, he'd easily become frustrated and abandon his efforts. After a few nights of panic-applying, Chris would shift into his morning snooze routine. Weeks would pass with no progress, until the three a.m. crisis mode would resume.

Attacking and avoiding, or fight and flight, is what our anxiety does best. Facing a monster, we assume the fetal position or wield a sword while blindfolded. When we keep charging at the problem and inevitably retreating from it, it's easy to forget that maybe we should try taking it out for a nice lunch instead. When we sit across the table from a challenge, suddenly it doesn't seem so intimidating.

I asked Chris to use words to describe a middle way between these 180-degree turns in productivity. Chris came up with words like observing, gathering, building, pacing, and so forth. We settled on "approaching." Approaching is the style of the differentiated job hunter, who is able to stay in contact with the challenge without becoming overwhelmed by his emotions. Approaching means doing your homework, knowing what you want, and understanding what it will take to get there.

Chris created a plan to approach the job hunt and find the middle ground between attacking and avoiding. Instead of working at three a.m. or setting his alarm for seven a.m., he scheduled a thirty-minute window each day at lunchtime. He would work longer if he was in a flow, but if he felt anxious, he allowed himself to stop. He could take a walk, or a hot shower, before he had to resume problem solving. He also sat down and defined the type of job he wanted, so that he wouldn't be distracted by easy pickings or discouraged by lengthy applications.

Before long, Chris was making small but solid progress. He was taking his problem out to lunch.

Attacking the Job Search	*Avoiding the Job Search*	*Approaching the Job Search*
• anxiously scrolling through job postings • applying to jobs you don't really want • working only when you feel panicked • taking shortcuts on applications	• not gathering appropriate data and resources • ruling out opportunities at first glance • waiting for the perfect moment to get started • shutting down when the process seems daunting	• focusing on the facts • knowing and following your principles • setting aside reasonable time for the process • sitting with the discomfort that good work takes time

The Trouble with Reassurance

The anxiety of the job search doesn't just mess with your career prospects—it also seeps into your relationships. When your friends and family sense that you're anxious, they begin to feel anxious as well. Rather than putting on their own oxygen mask, they will try to smash on yours with unhelpful advice or reassurance. This attempt to overfunction usually backfires, and you end up fighting with them or avoiding them.

This is exactly what happened with Chris. His well-meaning grad school friends forwarded him job postings that he had already seen. Other friends offered to proofread his nonexistent cover letters. He excused himself from social gatherings that would involve the inevitable career-focused small talk. Chris also continued to lie to his family. He knew that if his parents found out he was still searching, they would sound the alarm. His mother would reiterate her disapproval of his career path, and his father would grill him with financial questions.

As he slowly edged away from important relationships, Chris's girlfriend became the only place left to dump his worry. He peppered their conversations with pleas like, "Everything is going to be okay, right? I'll find a job eventually?" At first, she was happy to reassure him, but she quickly grew tired of calming him down. She'd snap, and then he'd accuse her of not being supportive. He asked her to make sure he'd applied to three jobs every week but grew cranky when she followed through.

When we're anxious about work, it's natural for us to turn to the people closest to use for reassurance. We want them to absolve us of our guilt or predict the future. But when we put the responsibility of our anxiety on others, we invite conflict into our relationships. People get tired of playing priest or fortune teller. We also become less capable of being objective when we ask others to tell us what we already know.

Chris continued to observe his anxious behaviors. He saw how he was distancing himself from important relationships and underfunctioning with his girlfriend. His challenge was to move closer to his loved ones and be more responsible for himself. People would inevitably try to calm him down, but the more he saw this behavior as automatic, the less he would respond defensively. But how should he respond? He made a plan by creating a set of principles for his relationships.

Chris's Principles
- I will communicate how I'm doing and not manage people's reactions.
- I will respond kindly but firmly when others try to take control of my job search.
- I will not ask my girlfriend to reassure me when I feel anxious about employment.
- I will take time to evaluate my progress rather than using other people's reactions as a metric.

Now Chris had a road map for navigating his reactivity around others. People were going to be anxious about his future, especially his parents. His job was to stay focused on himself and on managing his own emotions, rather than relying on his girlfriend to put out the fire.

Define Yourself in an Interview

By reclaiming the energy he used to avoid others, Chris was able to make some progress with the job search. Before long, he was getting responses and scheduling phone interviews with some big museums. But he never made it to the second round of interviews. He suspected that his anxiety was to blame.

It's easy to take a rejection, hand it to your anxiety, and say, "Knock yourself out!" Your anxiety will start spinning outlandish tales of how you are the worst human to have ever humaned. But when you stay plugged into reality rather than anxious fantasy, you'll find that rejection is no big deal. It's an opportunity to get more objective about yourself, to consider what you did well and what could use some time and attention. Success rarely affords the opportunity for self-improvement that rejection offers us, because why work on yourself when you got what you wanted?

When he took the time to evaluate his job interviews with more objectivity, Chris observed that his pseudo-self was hard at work. When an interviewer asked him about STEM education programs, he lied and said that he loved them. And in his attempt to pretend he had loads of STEM ideas for their museum, he took a giant faceplant. When another interviewer asked him about his current job, he gave some obscure answer about volunteering rather than admit he was a bartender.

BRING SELF, NOT PSEUDO-SELF,
TO AN INTERVIEW

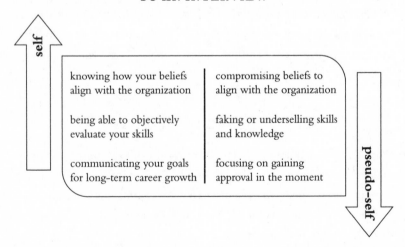

self	pseudo-self
knowing how your beliefs align with the organization	compromising beliefs to align with the organization
being able to objectively evaluate your skills	faking or underselling skills and knowledge
communicating your goals for long-term career growth	focusing on gaining approval in the moment

Chris was bending over backward trying to be the person he thought the interviewers wanted him to be. And he came across as inauthentic, inarticulate, and a little weird. He decided that it was okay to do research about his prospective employer, but he needed to study himself first. So he wrote down examples of projects that excited him. He got clear with himself about why he chose the field of museum education. He created a detailed list of skill deficits that he wanted to strengthen over the course of his career. Then he was able to research prospective employers with more clarity, tossing out the ones that wouldn't fit well with his goals and abilities.

Because he'd taken the time to study himself, Chris could stay focused on communicating these thoughts to an interviewer, instead of trying to manage their reactions toward him. It wasn't his job to mind read or jump through flaming hoops—it was to bring a clear definition of self to people who might hire him.

I suggested to Chris that he take this work further and broaden his definition of self outside of his career goals. He didn't know how long it would take him to find the job he wanted, and the richer his relationships and interests, the less likely his anxiety would try to take the wheel again. He agreed, and started moving closer to his friends and family. He also started volunteering for an after-school program.

The truth is that we're going to spend a lot of our lives waiting for the Next Big Thing, whether it's a job, a partner, or another dream. Who we are in the meantime is often what truly defines us, because so much of those things are out of our control. While you may not always get what you want, it's remarkable how simply calming down and defining yourself can get you a heck of a lot closer.

Your Questions

Observe

- When has my anxiety cycled between attacking and avoiding a goal?
- Do I ever become reactive when others try to fix a problem for me?
- How does my pseudo-self interfere with my career goals?

Evaluate

- How can I *approach* a goal I have, rather than attack or avoid?
- What would it look like for me to rely less on others for reassurance?
- What are my principles when it comes to applying and interviewing for a job?

Interrupt

- How can I manage my insecurities about a goal I have this week?
- What can I do now to more clearly define my career goals to myself?
- How can I broaden my definition of self while I work on something I really want?

Your Practice

Maybe you're not looking for a job right now. But like Chris, we're all at risk of charging half-assed toward a goal and then fleeing as if we're on fire. What would it look like for you to take a challenge "out to lunch"? Brainstorm some strategies so that working on this goal can be enjoyable and not a nightmare. Maybe you simply send an email or print out some information and then eat a cookie, because you deserve nice things. Perhaps you recruit a friend to work quietly with you. Once you dial down the anxiety, it's amazing how much energy you'll have to make some real progress.

CHAPTER 12

Your Terrible Boss

Details of your incompetence do not interest me.

—*Miranda Priestly*, The Devil Wears Prada

Morgan was living her own worst nightmare. She was a thirty-year-old lobbyist who had sent a text to a coworker complaining about her boss's random two a.m. emails. "I wouldn't mind getting middle of the night emails from Joanne if they actually made sense," she had texted. "And what's up with the giant font size? Is she trying to terrify us lol."

Morgan did end up terrified, because she had accidentally sent that text *to her boss* instead of her coworker. (I know!) Looking back, I'm impressed that she managed to make it to therapy at all instead of moving immediately to Siberia.

Morgan's boss called her into her office the next day. She gave a speech about professionalism, while a mortified Morgan melted into the carpet. She agreed with Joanne that in the future, she'd voice her concerns instead of complaining to coworkers. But after their meeting, Morgan grew bitter. She hated the holier-than-thou attitude her boss seemed to take. All she had done was sent one bad text—Joanne was the one who was too sensitive. Joanne was paranoid about getting fired by the big boss. Her favorite minions were always tattling on their coworkers to her. She rarely congratulated Morgan on a job well done. She didn't even know how to scan a document or Google a question, but she got paid twice as much! Morgan was anxiously focused on her boss, to say the least.

People say that a good boss or a bad boss can make or break a job experience. But perhaps there are fewer true villains than we like to think. Most bosses are simply imperfect, anxious humans like the rest of us. But because they get to decide our fate, we study them carefully for any sign of danger. This anxious focus can leave us tallying their flaws, and where we see fault, we find an opportunity to blame them for our anxiety.

Your Work Is an Emotional System

Just like your family, your workplace is a complex, emotional system. People are constantly acting and reacting in predictable patterns in an attempt to manage stress. You'll see those four strategies you've learned about over and over again: distance, conflict, over/under-functioning, and triangles.

A calm office full of mature people isn't going to be so dependent on these strategies. But in a workplace full of reactive and immature people, a simple event, like taking Sour Patch Kids out of the vending machine, can start a riot. Most people find that their workplace is somewhere in between these two extremes—you have some more differentiated people and some less differentiated people, and stressful events will come and go.

Morgan was so focused on her boss that she was stuck in cause-and-effect thinking. She was unable to see that her office was full of anxious humans, including herself. If Morgan could see the bigger relationship system, she wouldn't need a villain to blame for her anxiety. So I encouraged her to take her laser focus off of Joanne for a while and observe how the entire office functioned, especially on a bad day. Her conflict with her boss was just a small part of a bigger system trying its best to chug along. When she looked at the office with the eyes of a researcher instead of a disgruntled employee, she could see how these four strategies were holding the ship together.

Morgan's Observations

Distance: A coworker sent me an email with bad news even though we'd talked three times that day.

Conflict: Two people on my team refused to compromise on a presentation proposal.

Overfunctioning: I made a call for an annoying underling instead of letting them practice. Whoops!

Triangles: People are complaining that Bob from IT is too slow, when they could just check in with him.

All over the office, Morgan could see people avoiding, fighting, or bulldozing, when they should have been approaching, listening, and letting others learn. She was starting to see that Joanne's flaws weren't the problem—they were just symptoms of an anxious, imperfect work environment. Morgan also realized that she was also susceptible to immaturity, especially when she bristled around Joanne.

Unless you're the boss, you have little control over the amount of anxiety floating around your work. But good news—you can bump up your level of differentiation and boost your immunity to the stress. How do you do this? Say it with me—observe, evaluate, interrupt.

The Astronaut's View

Morgan could see how she was operating anxiously at work. But the texting fiasco had permanently altered her ability to be objective around her boss. Every time Joanne emailed her, disagreed with her in a meeting, or asked to meet with her, Morgan's brain screamed,

"*You are most definitely being fired!*" She struggled to differentiate between her thoughts and emotions.

You would think that this complete terror of being canned would make Morgan fall in line, be early to work, and execute her job with 100 percent precision. But it only did the opposite. Some days she struggled to make it in on time. She found herself arguing with people in staff meetings just for the sake of being contrary. Morgan had trouble concentrating on projects—what was the point if her boss hated her?

Though fear can be a motivator, it rarely turns us into our best selves. Morgan's actions at work were increasingly driven by her emotions, and her thinking desperately needed to take back the reins. I asked Morgan to think for a few minutes and tell me how an outside observer would describe how anxiety was influencing her actions.

"My anxiety says I'll be fired, and then I act as if that's true," she said. "So there's no point in trying if it's already over."

Acting from a anxiety-based perspective often means you're relying on inaccurate data. If you can zoom out and describe what's happening in the relationship system, then you can be more objective. I call this "taking the astronaut's view." Because from space, most of our problems seem manageable.

Let's Practice!

Scenario: Your boss is a little short with you in a phone call.
Ground View: He hates me. Time to polish that résumé!
Astronaut's View: My boss is a human who will have anxious days.

Scenario: Your supervisor invites another colleague out to lunch instead of you.
Ground View: I can't believe those monsters are going to eat tacos without me.

Astronaut's View: I'm feeling reactive because I'm on the outside of a triangle right now.

Scenario: Your boss is micromanaging your work on a project.
Ground View: Why can't this woman get a hobby!
Astronaut's View: Some people overfunction when they're stressed. It's not personal.

Taking the astronaut's view, Morgan saw herself as a slightly neurotic but decent employee who was letting her anxiety get in the way of a better performance. She wasn't the office pariah, and Joanne wasn't plotting to get rid of her. If she had wanted to do so, wouldn't that embarrassing text have been reason enough? Their conflict wasn't an epic battle—it was just another sign of an anxious work system. Joanne might continue to be reactive around her, but Morgan was absolutely capable of responding with more maturity. As she mentally floated above the office, Morgan could see the value in gaining some objectivity.

Mentorship or Worship?

Like a good astronaut, Morgan continued to observe how her anxiety affected her behavior at work. She watched how she used distance to manage the tension between herself and Joanne. She sent emails to avoid conversations. She asked the big boss questions that should have been directed toward Joanne. Morgan knew that she needed to bridge the distance between herself and her boss. If she didn't have closer access to Joanne's thoughts, her bitter feelings and fear of getting fired would never be resolved. But Morgan wasn't thrilled with the idea of increased communication.

"When I took this job, I thought she'd be a mentor to me," she complained. "But she rarely encourages me or tells me I've done a good job."

When we talked about her history with authority figures, Morgan saw how she relied on the praise of professors, coaches, and bosses for her own sense of self-worth. If she wasn't being actively praised, then she assumed that she was doing something wrong. When she had a boss who fawned over her, she performed wonderfully. When she didn't, she became irritable and quickly jumped ship. She could see the pattern repeating. If she didn't intervene, she was going to get herself fired or end up quitting out of spite. And her bank account couldn't afford either.

Mentors are wonderful. But relying too much on their praise can keep us from building a stronger sense of self. External praise only temporarily puffs up the pseudo-self. When your supervisor offers little to no praise, you might find yourself becoming anxious or resentful. Morgan began to realize that Joanne might never be her cheerleader. But she found the work worthwhile, and she didn't want to bail. We considered what it might look like for her to not treat her boss like an approval vending machine, but as a fellow human and a collaborator who also enjoyed the work.

Often my clients tell me they're looking for a mentor at work when they're really saying, "I want someone to worship me for the wunderkind that I am." Or if they're a supervisor looking for a mentee, they want a mini-me who will worship them. But these kinds of relationships are based on emotions, not ideas. A true mentorship is a meeting of the minds, not a meeting of the feelings. And it can withstand much more than a passing storm of disagreement.

A mentorship built on emotions:
- is a roller coaster of highs and lows
- keeps you dependent on praise
- prevents you from evaluating yourself
- makes disagreement unbearable
- is likely to end in conflict

A mentorship built on thinking:
- is low in anxiety
- stays focused on goals
- isn't threatened by outsiders
- helps you evaluate yourself
- can survive disagreement

Morgan set aside her cravings for approval and began to initiate more conversations with Joanne. Rather than trying to please or provoke her boss, Morgan simply shared her thinking and tried to listen to Joanne's as well. By taking the focus off of Joanne and putting it back onto her own thinking, Morgan found that she suddenly looked forward to their conversations. She might never feel as euphoric around Joanne as she did around her college professors, but she also knew that she wouldn't feel as cranky or fearful when they disagreed, or when Joanne gave challenging feedback.

Morgan also began to notice that her boss seemed to calm down as well. She sent Morgan fewer midnight emails, gave face-to-face feedback, and listened carefully to Morgan's thoughts. This was further proof to Morgan that when she became the person she wanted to be, everyone's anxiety went down a little. She might not be the boss, but she could certainly be the calmest person in the room.

Your Questions

Observe

- How has anxiety affected my relationship with a boss or supervisor?
- Which of the four strategies do I use to manage stress at work?
- Have I ever become too dependent on praise from a boss or mentor?

Evaluate

- How would a more mature version of myself operate at work?
- What principles can keep me calm around my superiors at work?
- In what areas of work do I need to zoom out and take the astronaut's view?

Interrupt

- How can I stay focused on myself when I'm tempted to label my boss as the problem?
- How can I remember to observe anxious patterns at my work?
- What do I think is the first step in building a more mature relationship with my boss?

Your Practice

Most of us have been in a mentor relationship that's based more on feeling than thinking. Maybe you got jealous when your basketball coach turned their focus to a new rising star. Perhaps you lost all your motivation when a favorite boss left for maternity leave. Consider the mentors in your life right now or the mentors you'd like to have. Take a moment to write down some ideas about how you can make this relationship a meeting of the minds rather than a meeting of emotions. Do you need to be more honest when you disagree with them? Should you write down your own thinking before you ask them for advice? Do you need to start acting more like an adult instead of a golden retriever who hasn't been petted in three weeks? The more maturity you bring to a relationship with a mentor, the more you're likely to enjoy it.

CHAPTER 13

Procrastination and Productivity

> There's nothing we can't do if we work hard, never
> sleep, and shirk all other responsibilities in our lives.
>
> —*Leslie Knope*, Parks and Recreation

Martha's New Year's resolution was to start therapy, but she didn't show up until April. In her defense, she came in to talk about her trouble with deadlines. Martha worked remotely as a pop culture reporter for a popular website. Five years into her career, she no longer felt that she was soaring toward a successful one. It felt more like flailing toward mediocrity.

Martha's biggest challenge was procrastination. Her job had become uninteresting, and she would delay rewrites on an article or interview. She would wait too long, until she convinced herself that there wasn't enough time left for an article to be great. This generated anxiety, which further fueled the procrastination. She asked for extensions often, and her once generous editors were growing frustrated.

Martha's brain was like a car alarm. If she didn't shut the worry off in time, it would kick up to the next level of frantic wailing. "Are you even a writer if you can't write?" it would ask. Super helpful.

Why do we procrastinate on tasks that aren't life-threatening? You would think that after a few five a.m. paper submissions in college, we'd learn that living on the edge isn't that great. I don't know about other countries, but the capacity for Americans to be simultaneously great at procrastinating and obsessed with productivity is comical.

It doesn't help that humans are terrible at estimating how long a task will take us. Psychologists Daniel Kahneman and Amos Tversky call this the "planning fallacy." We assume we won't have any difficulties, we delay getting started, and this optimism gets us into trouble. Ask someone what's the latest possible date they'll complete a task, and the odds are they won't be finished by that date.

But Martha's problem wasn't a matter of optimism. Like most human challenges, it originated in her relationships.

Procrastination Is a Relationship Problem

Unless you're a doomsday prepper living off the grid, your job is relational. Therefore, procrastination is often a relationship problem. Assuming that a problem or symptom exists independent of a relationship system is to ignore what it means to be human. How you react to your colleagues, your family, and the larger world can tell you a lot about how you end up anxiously stalling on a project. Rather than observing how we function in relationship to others, we end up labeling our productivity problems as personality flaws. This leaves us feeling ashamed and stuck.

Martha certainly saw her procrastination as a character flaw. She had read many time-management books but always failed to apply the ideas in them. She believed that if she could teach herself to get up at five a.m. or abandon her reality show addiction, she would unlock the superhero power of mass production. But the transformation never seemed to happen.

Martha was so busy shaming herself that she failed to see the bigger picture. She needed to take the astronaut's view, zoom high above herself, and observe that her procrastination was not a solo endeavor. There were other people editing, reading, and responding to her work. Because she worked at home, it was easy to forget that there were other humans in the game.

I encouraged Martha to think about her procrastination as a relationship problem. She started by listing all the people who inhabited her brain when she felt anxious about her work. She worried what her editors thought about giving her extensions, since she couldn't gauge their reactions through email. She wanted to impress a new girl she was seeing. She didn't want to disappoint her sweet grandmother, whose house was wallpapered with years of her bylines. If she was being honest, she also wanted to look good in front of Twitter followers she'd never even met.

By focusing on the reactions of others, Martha had invited an entire audience of people to watch her write a first draft. It was like sight-reading a cello piece at Carnegie Hall when you don't even play the cello. No wonder her brain shut down and refused to work when she had an assignment.

There are so many ways that our relationships influence our level of productivity. Here are just a few:

Anxiety in relationships can lead to:
- worrying about how people will respond to your work
- slacking when someone else will do it for you
- distancing yourself from those who expect you to do well
- pretending that you're more capable than you are
- focusing on getting approval instead of developing ideas

People who are less emotionally mature, or less differentiated, tend to be more other-focused in their work. Dr. Bowen proposed that less differentiated people were more reactive to praise or criticism. They used up all their energy trying to look good, and there wasn't much left for getting stuff done.

Less differentiated people also tend to procrastinate because they often imagine they are disappointing others. If you imagine that a friend is upset with you, you might delay calling them back. If you imagine that your boss will be impatient, you might lie about how quickly you can finish a project. If you imagine that Grandma will be disappointed, you might forget all the times you've pulled off the same task with great success. Martha's imagination had taken over and was doing all of the above.

How do you focus less on disappointing others? You might try to avoid them, but this rarely works. If you don't believe me, consider how much time you've spent trying to impress strangers on social media, to prove a dead relative wrong, or to beat that high school nemesis who always outdid you. Just because you're not talking to someone doesn't mean that you're not in a relationship with them. And distancing yourself from people will only give your imagination more space to paint a negative picture.

So rather than distancing herself, Martha needed to move *closer* to the people who were inhabiting her brain: her editors, her new girlfriend, and Grandma. She realized that if these relationships lived or died by her ability to be impressive, she was signing up for a lifetime of anxious procrastinating. So Martha began inching closer. She initiated more conversations with her editors about big ideas and their own lives. She was honest with her girlfriend about her procrastination problems and her career fears. She asked her grandmother about her own decision to give up a career to start a family. By moving closer, Martha was beginning to see that she was surrounded by humans, not just fans or critics. It felt really good.

Schedule Time for Curiosity

Though it might seem scary at first, moving closer to important people can do a lot to lower your anxiety in the long run. The less focused you are on their reactions, the more energy you'll have to pursue your goals. So where should your focus be, if not on other people?

Martha had been so determined to be impressive that she'd forgotten why she'd become a journalist in the first place. Without that guiding passion, she became more concerned with what other people thought (or what she imagined they thought). Because she was constantly behind on her assignments, Martha had begun to deny herself pleasures that increased her productivity. "You can't get excited about anything until you finish this article!" she told herself. You can imagine how well that worked.

It's easy to forget that the first step in doing a thing is to get interested in the thing. As a therapist, if I'm not curious about my client's challenges, then I'm going to be zero help. Curiosity is a big part of productivity, but our anxiety will thwart it at every turn. Our anxiety wants us to skip straight to the doing so that the problem can be solved. This is simply the job of our anxiety—to calm things down with fast responses. But our challenge is to override that autopilot response with a slower, more thoughtful strategy.

Martha could see she would have a boring and stressful career if she didn't make space for curiosity every week. She took the time to write down some ideas for how she could stay curious about her work.

Martha's Ideas for Staying Curious
- Listen to podcasts while I commute.
- Hop into a museum exhibit on my lunch break.
- Schedule time with friends who like to talk about big ideas.

- Attend author talks at my local bookstore.
- Keep observing the relationships that make me anxious.

At first, Martha was skeptical about letting herself have fun. Weren't these just more ways to procrastinate on writing? How would she know the difference between engaging curiosity and just plain slacking off? To solve this problem, she decided that she would simply allot herself a certain amount of time each week to fuel her brain. This time was sacred, and it was only for regenerating energy, not for producing content.

Over time, Martha began to prioritize thinking as much as she valued the "doing" of her job. When she made space for curiosity, there was still plenty of time to do the hard work.

Monster of the Week

Martha had begun to take the focus off of others, and she was finding time to jump-start her brain. But she still had to sit down and be a journalist. When she did, she often found her old demons waiting for her. Martha knew that she was perfectly capable of writing a seven-hundred-word article explaining which famous Chris was the greatest of all time. But for some reason she lost all faith in her abilities when she faced a blank page.

When Martha examined her fear, she found that her anxiety tended to take a long-term focus. It wasn't asking her, "What if you picked the wrong Chris? What if it's really Hemsworth and not Evans?" It was saying things like, "Do you think it's too late for you to really be successful?" Or "What if you get phased out? A robot could probably do this job in twenty years." Or her least favorite, "Look, here's someone five years younger than you who's ten times more successful!"

Getting stuff done is not a long-term problem. It's a short-term, task-by-task affair. In her book *Bird by Bird*, Anne Lamott explains how she has a one-inch picture frame on her desk to remind her to stay focused on a small piece of a much bigger story. Martha needed a similar strategy to stay focused on short-term tasks. Martha was a pop culture expert, so I compared her dilemma to a TV phrase known as "Monster of the Week." On many science fiction or fantasy shows, there are filler weeks when a villain or monster is defeated by the end of the episode. Not every episode in the show is about the bigger story, but the characters are always developing, monster by monster. I asked Martha to think about what it would look like to set aside her thoughts about her career trajectory for a bit and just focus on her weekly monsters. Getting one article edited or finishing a set of interviews or pitching a few new ideas to her editor were tasks that needed her attention. Bigger questions could wait.

Every day of your career does not have to be big-picture focused. If you're an actor and you get up every morning and stare at a picture of Viola Davis while you eat your Cheerios, you're going to end up anxious and exhausted. It's important to take the time to write down your goals, but they aren't going anywhere. If you've been paying attention, you know that it's much more effective to have *principles* guiding you rather than outcomes you might not be able to control. Goals tell you why you're working, but principles tell you how to approach each day and each monster.

So every Monday, Martha picked a single monster that needed to be zapped by the end of the week. She made sure to prioritize the ugliest, most annoying task. If her anxiety tried to distract her with some doomsday career scenario or shiny long-term goal, she stopped, took a deep breath, and asked herself what was the next step in finishing the monster. And she found herself defeating the monsters, one by one.

If you've ever watched *The X-Files*, you know that some of the best episodes are about those monsters of the week. Martha found that the same was true for her work—she felt her skills sharpen on articles that once seemed routine, or she got excited about a new idea when she tackled a daunting subject. Big success is great, but so is the feeling you get when you show up every week and do what needs to be done. Slay those weekly monsters, and be proud of yourself.

Your Questions

Observe

- What people in my life do I desperately want to impress?
- How does my work anxiety keep me from being curious?
- When does worrying about long-term goals distract me from weekly tasks?

Evaluate

- How is procrastination a relationship problem for me?
- What would it look like for me to live a more curious life?
- What principles could guide me through my weekly tasks?

Interrupt

- What's one small change I can make to lower procrastination anxiety?
- How would I like to make space for curiosity this month?
- What's one monster I would like to focus on defeating this week?

Your Practice

If you struggle with procrastination, chances are your anxiety wants you to impress everyone and meet your goals as quickly as possible.

So how can you interrupt your anxiety and do the opposite? How can you be less dependent on their praise? How can you make time for curiosity, and keep a steady pace of monster crushing? Reread one section from this chapter, and write down some ideas about how you'd like to lower your anxiety about productivity.

CHAPTER 14

Switching Careers

> **Well, I've narrowed it down to two possibilities: yes and no.**
>
> —Chidi Anagonye, The Good Place

Anthony had a dream that one day he would make less money. Seriously. The big fancy lawyer life was killing this thirty-one-year-old, and he wanted to get off the ride. But he still had law school debt, his wife was a social worker, and day care for their two-year-old son cost roughly $6 billion. Anthony's life revolved around billable hours, and he resented having to show up on weekends and delay one family vacation after another.

What was the point in making good money if you couldn't even enjoy it? Senior colleagues encouraged him that if he put in a few more years, he'd have more time and even more money. A few more years? He didn't know if he could make it to Friday.

When Anthony came to therapy, he explained that his real dream was to quit his job, go back to grad school, and become an art therapist. Late one night when he was battling insomnia, he had watched a documentary about kids in Africa who'd lost their parents to AIDS. They'd learn to heal from trauma through art and storytelling. As the credits rolled, Anthony searched online for local art therapy programs. The next morning at breakfast, while their son shoved oatmeal up his nose, he told his wife his plan. Her response was kind but firm. There was no way in hell that they'd survive a career jump. Anthony sulked for a bit and shoved the plan into the back of his brain. But the idea just wouldn't die.

Gallup has named millennials the "Job-Hopping Generation" because they're three times more likely to change jobs in a year than any other generation before them. They're blamed for being less engaged at work, but perhaps it's because they simply want to do something worthwhile. But how do know when a leap is right, or just a distraction? Do you scratch the itch, or do you just grow a beard or start a podcast?

Anxiety can keep you from making a career leap, but it can also push you out of the plane before you're ready. Before you wonder what color your parachute could be, perhaps consider whether you even have one.

Fantasy Versus Reality

Most career switches start as innocent daydreaming. A 2017 report found that television shows had influenced 39 percent of British millennials when making their career choice. Fictional role models are wonderful, and they can provide powerful representation for young people. But they can also lead to disappointment. Half the people of DC are here because they wanted to reenact *The West Wing* but ended up in a *Veep* episode. I wonder how many surgical residents became angry when they discovered they wouldn't be having as much sex as *Grey's Anatomy* characters.

Fictional careers tug on our emotions with compelling drama and a great soundtrack. But the fantasy rarely shows you all the paperwork, the boring meetings, or the grad school debt. Choosing a career isn't a decision void of emotion. But when it's a choice based entirely in emotion, we're more likely to rely on fantasy than reality. Anthony was one step closer to reality because he'd been inspired by a documentary. But when I asked him how much he knew about art therapy jobs, he admitted that he hadn't done much research. He had the dream, but he had no facts.

Anthony's fantasy excited him, but the potential nightmare of a bad decision kept him glued to the law firm. He needed to sweep away all the emotions for a while and see what facts were left. For his therapy homework, I asked him to write down both his fantasy scenario and his nightmare scenario if he made a career switch. Here's what he wrote:

Anthony's Fantasy: Every morning I hop out of bed, throw on casual clothes, and drive to a giant, brightly lit studio full of unlimited art supplies. I'm working with underserved, well-behaved teenagers, and I solve all their problems with a few rounds of drama therapy or collage making. Each day I leave feeling good about myself, and I arrive home just in time to help my son with his homework.

Anthony's Nightmare: I'm stuck in some closet in a crumbling nonprofit with nothing but a box of broken crayons and a mountain of paperwork. I'm ineffective at my job. I spend all my time commuting, because I've had to move my family out to nowheresville so our budget can support my pipe dreams.

It's funny how one brain can dance anxiously between two completely opposite outcomes. When he saw these scenarios on paper, Anthony suspected that his experience as an art therapist would be somewhere between a blue-jean-wearing Messiah and a man buried alive by case notes. But he could take these scenarios and use them to clarify the decision-making process. He needed to sift his dreams and fears and see what values fell out. Here were the values that stood out to him.

Anthony's Values
- feeling comfortable at work
- spending more time with clients than paperwork
- having my own space to be creative
- working with a well-resourced organization
- working hours that allow me to spend time with my son

Now things were getting real. Anthony had a concrete list of aims that felt attainable and reasonable. By clarifying his values, he wasn't crushing his dreams. He was simply negotiating between fantasy and nightmare to find what he really cared about. Now he just needed to figure out whether a career in art therapy could give him what he wanted.

The Trap of All or Nothing

When you're ready to make a big change in life, it's easy to get impatient. Combine this impatience with anxiety, and you're likely to act without thinking. Maybe you decide to eat healthier and throw away everything in your fridge. Or you want to dress like a New Yorker, so you donate everything in your closet that isn't black. But then Friday rolls around, and you just want to wear purple and eat frosting right out of the container.

The more he dreamed about a creative life, the more antsy Anthony became. He feared that if he didn't start making moves, he would lose momentum and stay stuck at the law firm.

Have you heard of the famous Marshmallow Test? Psychologists offered children a choice: they could get one marshmallow immediately or get two if they could wait fifteen minutes. Anthony was facing a similar challenge. He could probably start an art therapy program within months if he quit his job, took out loans, and asked his wife to take on more responsibility. But what treats would he be missing by impulsively grasping for a new life?

Anthony needed to interrupt his anxiety long enough to make a real plan for himself. He needed to recognize the lies that his anxiety would use to trick him into acting quickly. Once he identified the lie, he needed to dig deep and use his thinking to be more objective. His anxiety loved to tell him that if he didn't act quickly, he would soon be too old to change careers. "That's ridiculous," his thinking would respond. "It's not like I want to be an athlete or a pop star. I'm allowed to change directions in life whenever I like."

Anthony was starting to realize that his career was not a poker game—he didn't have to choose between folding or going all in. He could dip his toes in the water and test out a different kind of life without putting his future at risk. His anxiety was going to hate this strategy, but it would just have to deal.

What are some of the common lies that your anxiety will tell when it wants you to jump without thinking or freeze in place? How can you stay objective when it tries to frighten you?

Let's Practice!

Anxiety: You will be here until the building crumbles down around you.

Thinking: I can make a strategic leap when I've decided it's right and smart.

Anxiety: The grass is always greener. You're dumb for thinking you'll be happier!

Thinking: I am capable of evaluating what's best for me at this time.

Anxiety: Just keep taking out student loans until you die! Take that, government!

Thinking: Being financially irresponsible will only make me more anxious in the long run.

Anxiety: You're a quitter, and you always have been! Remember oboe lessons?

Thinking: Okay, seriously, anxiety? There are like six professional oboists in the world.

The Smart Leap

While he kept his anxiety down, Anthony ran the numbers over and over. He looked at his bank account. He checked stats about the availability and average salary of art therapy jobs. His discussed various strategies with his wife, but they just couldn't seem to come up with a plan where a big career change would leave them both happy and solvent.

Anthony was starting to question whether a career switch would make him happy, or whether it was just a temporary fix for calming down a stressful life. As a child, he'd watched his father hop between relationships and elaborate money-making schemes. But the temporary euphoria of a shiny new endeavor always seemed to fade into depression. Anthony wanted his own son to have a father who pursued his passions but also honored his commitments and provided for his family. Ultimately, he valued this legacy more than another turn at grad school.

A few months passed, and Anthony found himself turning back to the list of values he had sifted out of his dreams and nightmares. Perhaps there was still a way to make space for creativity and for his family. After talking with his wife, he approached his boss and asked if it were possible for him to bill fewer hours each quarter. And he was surprised to find that this was absolutely an option.

As far as I know, Anthony never became an art therapist. But he started volunteering for an art program at his church, and he was planning a vacation with his family. These joys calmed his anxious mind, and he started to enjoy being a lawyer again. He had made a small but smart leap, without blowing up his life.

How to Take a Smart Leap
- Take the time to define your values and principles.
- Acknowledge that honoring these principles may lead to a different outcome.
- Work on managing anxiety before you make any decisions.
- Be willing to sit with the discomfort that smart change takes time.
- Understand that people will have anxious reactions to your decision.

If you're thinking about switching careers, your story may not be like Anthony's. Maybe you do need to make a big move, turn in your notice, or spend a few more years in graduate school. It's not so much about what you choose. It's about who's doing the choosing. Is it your anxiety, looking for a quick way to avoid stress? Or is it your best thinking? There is more than one way to make space for what you value in life. Some people are lucky enough to find it at work, and some people are mature enough to think outside the box.

Your Questions

Observe

- Has stress ever made me fantasize about a career change?
- Has anxiety ever tempted me to act too quickly on a career decision?
- Has anxiety ever kept me frozen in a job I hated?

Evaluate

- What might my career fantasies and nightmares tell me about what I really value?
- How might I practice managing anxiety while making a big decision?
- What wisdom would I like to remember when making a big career decision?

Interrupt

- How can I make more space in my life for my career values?
- How can I recognize anxious thought patterns about my career?
- What's an upcoming decision where I can practice making a mature plan?

Your Practice

Are you curious to see what values your fantasy and nightmare job scenarios may reveal? Take a few minutes, and describe each of them on paper. Separate what's pure fantasy and nightmare from what's attainable. Consider how these values can be accessed in your current life, and which ones might require more long-term changes. Maybe you can't quit your job today, but you can start living a life that reflects what's really important to you.

CHAPTER 15

Being a Leader

> **So live as if you were living already for the second time and as if you had acted the first time as wrongly as you are about to act now.**
>
> —*Viktor Frankl, Man's Search for Meaning*

Janelle had a problem—she was too good at her job. She was a thirty-five-year-old social worker who'd been promoted to the position of clinical director at a women's shelter. The last two directors hadn't lasted six months, but she welcomed the challenge. Janelle was the oldest of five siblings, and she tended to thrive in chaotic situations.

Her first week on the job, she went full-on Boss Mode. She scheduled one-on-one time with her staff to improve their record-keeping skills. She popped into client appointments to make sure that staff were meeting their needs. She planned and ran a training that reinforced ethical standards the staff was ignoring. Janelle had fantasized about playing captain of a well-run ship, but the reality felt like mutiny. People showed up late to meetings and seemed blasé about her suggestions. And she was 97 percent certain that her former colleagues were now bitching about her in the break room.

You would think that high achievers like Janelle make natural leaders. They thrive on clocking long hours, picking up new skills, and dunking on goals ahead of schedule. But the test of leadership has one variable that can spoil any streak of success—other humans. When you're put in charge of other people, you're entering into the complexity of a relationship system that simply refuses to be tamed. It might not be *Game of Thrones*, but you will encounter resistance and the anxiety of others. This can be terrifying or infuriating if you're a new leader.

Janelle was learning that her impressive tactics as a follower simply didn't translate into stellar leadership. Her anxious desire to succeed had gotten her a promotion, but it failed her when it bumped up against the anxieties of her new staff. She needed a different strategy for being a leader, and she needed it fast.

Overfunctioning Isn't Leading

Janelle was smart—she knew that she must lead by example. She needed to nurture the talents of her staff because it was impossible for her to do everyone's job. But this thinking flew out the window on a stressful day. Janelle wasn't used to leaving tasks undone. It was difficult to prioritize relationships over the workload. She wanted her staff to keep well-organized files. But when a big audit loomed, it was easier to organize them herself. Why chase people down to do a half-hearted job? She also wanted her staff to manage their own schedules. But she kept texting them to make sure they weren't taking extra-long lunch breaks.

Janelle's anxious focus on her staff didn't encourage them to shape up. In fact, it made them less competent. Her constant monitoring stressed them out, which led to sloppier work. "What am I supposed to do?" she wondered. "Just kick back and let them do a terrible job?"

In therapy, we talked about Janelle's habit of overfunctioning for others when she became anxious. It was her go-to strategy for dealing with her big family. Janelle's mother had died when she was a teenager, making her the matriarch of the family. She was often giving advice to her siblings, mediating disagreements, and providing financial support. Janelle felt comfortable being over-responsible for her siblings, but at work it only made her queasy. Worrying about her staff made it difficult to focus on her own responsibilities. She let deadlines slip, and all her creative energy evaporated.

Burnout is common among leaders because the lines between their responsibilities and other people's begin to blur. People are given leadership roles because they've achieved a certain level of competence. But when they're given a front row seat to watch others do the work less effectively or differently, they become anxious. It's like watching your grandmother try to use her new remote control. The quickest way to calm yourself is to swoop in and simply take over.

You might be an overfunctioning leader if you:
- anxiously observe your followers
- offer help before someone asks for help
- struggle to delegate challenging tasks
- have trouble maintaining boundaries between work and home
- sound overly apologetic in your emails
- enjoy doing other people's work more than your own

Don't beat yourself up if this sounds like you. Remember that overfunctioning and underfunctioning are reciprocal, and that both people participate equally. Many of Janelle's staff were more than happy to let her do their work for them. They began to act less competent, which reinforced her impulse to jump in and take over.

Janelle was finding that her overfunctioning was only a temporary solution for reducing anxiety. In the long run, she had signed herself up for more work than she could ever do. Her staff would never become more effective as long as she was anxiously focused on them.

She needed to learn to sit with her anxiety so that everyone would calm down over time.

Get Comfortable with Being Uncomfortable

Overfunctioning wasn't the only anxious strategy that Janelle used in her new job. She found herself slowly inching away from staff who were difficult and reactive. Janelle was particularly allergic to one employee. Susan was at least twenty years older, and she'd worked at the shelter much longer than Janelle. Susan worked wonderfully with their clients, but she skirted policies and hated keeping records. When Janelle began implementing new standards in staff meetings, Susan became antagonistic or played a game on her cell phone.

Susan made Janelle anxious as hell. She dreaded their one-on-one meetings so much that she began to let Susan skip them or came up with excuses herself. No previous leader had managed to get Susan to cooperate, so why rock the boat? Janelle sent emails to Susan addressing problems that should have been solved face-to-face. She let Susan turn in paperwork late or cut ethical corners with her clients. All of Janelle's energy was directed toward keeping their relationship calm.

Most leaders simply don't have time to meet with everyone as often as they'd like. But rather than decreasing contact with the most competent people, they begin to distance themselves from the most anxious people. As you've learned, distance is a great short-term strategy for keeping everyone calm. But when a leader values a temporary truce over solid relationships, they're only delaying conflict. They're forfeiting the mission of the group or organization. When a leader avoids anxious people, they're also inadvertently playing favorites with calmer people in the group. This is likely to make an anxious person even more reactive.

A mature leader spends the most time with the most anxious people in their group. Sounds pretty terrible, right? But the only way you can ever learn to stay calm and thoughtful around anxious people is to spend time with them. This cannot be accomplished through email or text or by surrounding yourself with a room full of buffer humans. Or by triangling in another supervisor or an HR representative (though this may be necessary at times). If your anxiety shouts, "Run!," you might need to get more comfortable with being uncomfortable as a leader.

I asked Janelle to estimate how anxious Susan was on a scale from 1 to 100. "Easily an 85," she replied without a blink. When they occupied the same room, Janelle's anxiety shot up to an 85 as well. She immediately tried to leave or make Susan happy. It hadn't occurred to her to simply manage her own anxiety. She could take a deep breath or make some casual conversation with Susan. If she could bring her anxiety down to a 50, then Susan might calm down as well. Now Janelle had a plan. It would take a lot of practice, but she had given herself a fair shot at interrupting this anxious standoff with Susan.

Good Leaders Can Self-Regulate

By being over-responsible for everyone and over-focused on their anxiety, Janelle had forgotten her number 1 responsibility—*herself.*

Self-regulation is the ability to manage your own emotions and think for yourself. And it's an essential quality of any differentiated leader. Without the ability to self-regulate, you're at the mercy of the group and all its stressors. You'll be pulled into those automatic strategies of distancing, overfunctioning, and so on and lose the ability to act from the inside out.

Learning to self-regulate is about turning inward. I asked Janelle to write down some of the problems she faced as the boss. She needed to consider how other-focus got her into trouble and how self-focus could get her out of it. Here's an example of her thinking:

Problem: A new intake procedure at the shelter is making the staff irritable.

Other-focus: I try to convince everyone that it'll make their work easier.

Self-focus: I take time to clarify this decision to myself. I communicate the changes to staff without managing their reactions.

Janelle could see that trying to please or convince her staff was an impossible task. She needed to step back, think, and then communicate. Managing the emotions of the group was not her responsibility.

Let's Practice!

Let's take a look at how shifting from other-focus to self-focus can help you be a calmer, more effective leader.

Problem: You're not invited to a staff member's holiday party.

Other-focus: You stalk them on Facebook, looking for ideas to get them to like you.

Self-focus: You invite people to the type of gatherings you'd like to attend.

Problem: Everyone always blames Tom for low sales numbers.

Other-focus: You treat Tom as if he's the plague incarnate.

Self-focus: You zoom out and see your part in reinforcing Tom's low performance.

Problem: Your friend group always talks about Kardashian antics.

Other-focus: You criticize them for not having passionate conversations about big ideas.

Self-focus: You bring up what's important to you and let people respond however they like.

Problem: Your siblings always get plastered at family gatherings.
Other-focus: You replace half the vodka in the bottle with water.
Self-focus: You stay calm and explain that you will not debate with them when they've been drinking.

There are opportunities for leadership at work, at home, and everywhere you go. Self-focus isn't about assuming everything is your fault. It's about keeping your attention on what you can control and giving others an opportunity to follow. Because you cannot make anyone do anything they don't want to do.

Janelle was beginning to realize that she would never be able to make all of her staff happy with every decision she made. She would never be able to convince people to operate exactly the way she wanted them to operate. But it didn't matter because she was the boss. She needed to turn her attention back to herself—by being her own boss, she would be a more effective leader. She needed guiding principles to help her be the leader she wanted to be, instead of the version her anxiety thrust upon her. Here are some of the principles she wrote down.

Janelle's Leadership Principles
- I need to stay calm instead of calming everyone else.
- I can share my thinking, but I can't make people agree with it.
- I need to act mature instead of forcing maturity on other people.
- I can move closer to anxious people instead of avoiding them.
- I can step back and let people complete their own work.

These are such simple ideas, but so hard to implement! These principles would likely keep Janelle busy for the rest of her career. But at least she knew where to start.

Vive la Résistance

Every leader will face resistance from the group. You will have to communicate ideas or decisions that might not be popular. You might even face outright mutiny. This is why focusing on yourself is so important. If you've been relying on the praise, approval, or agreement of the group to direct you (aka those pseudo-self boosters), then you will do whatever it takes not to lose this support. This could mean sacrificing your principles and your thinking about what is best for a group or organization. But if you've taken the time to develop your own thinking, then it's a little bit easier to hold firm when you face pushback.

Leaders who live in fear of pushback are going to be sensitive to every frown and whisper they get from the group. They're going to waste all their energy trying to read other people's thoughts instead of communicating their own. But if you can accept the inevitability of resistance, and understand that it's the relationship system doing its thing, then you are going to be less reactive. You might even be able to welcome resistance as an opportunity to work on being a more differentiated leader. It's your chance to communicate your thinking but also be flexible enough to listen to the thoughts of others without becoming defensive.

Janelle feared pushback, but she was tired of letting her anxiety take the lead. She took some time to get really clear with herself about her principles for being a leader. She decided what she was willing to do and not do for her staff. And the next time she rolled out a new set of procedures for the shelter, she waited for the pushback. And sure enough, her staff began to gripe. Janelle quickly shut it down. "I'm happy to hear or read any suggestions you have, but not right now. Please send me a detailed email or schedule a one-on-one meeting with me," she said. "But tomorrow, this is our new procedure. It's your responsibility to ask for help if need it. Otherwise I'm going to assume that you are capable of implementing it."

Janelle didn't magically become an impenetrable boss lady who stopped wanting to be liked. She was still a human who craved approval and harmony as much as anyone. But she was starting to learn how to set those cravings aside when they conflicted with her principles. She might feel insecure, but she was beginning to trust her thinking more than her anxiety.

I hope that Janelle found other ways to work on being a more differentiated leader in her family and other areas of life. Whether you're the boss or the intern, the matriarch or the youngest sibling, there are opportunities to step up and be the calmest person in the room. And to be a little bit freer of the anxious forces that govern so many of our relationships.

Your Questions

Observe

- Do I ever become over-responsible for others when I'm the leader?
- Have I ever avoided anxious or difficult people whom I supervise?
- When has my desire to be liked gotten in the way of being a good leader?

Evaluate

- How do my actions as a leader contradict my ideas about leadership?
- How might I learn to be more self-regulated as a leader?
- What principles do I want to guide me in a leadership role?

Interrupt

- Are there any current patterns of overfunctioning or distancing I'd like to interrupt?
- What are upcoming opportunities for me to test out my leadership principles?
- How can I make space each week to prioritize managing my own anxiety?

Your Practice

Where do you see potential to be a leader in your life? You don't have to be the boss to be an example of calmness or maturity to others. Pick one arena of life where you'd like to lead more, and be honest about how you try to control others rather than yourself. Are you quick to overfunction for a colleague who is just too freaking slow? Do you lecture a younger sibling about getting their life together? Are you always playing the peacemaker in a group of squabbling friends? Make a plan detailing how you can step back, calm down, and go back into these relationships as a leader. What would it look like to tolerate a little bit of anxiety and inspire people to be more responsible for themselves?

Let's Review Part 3!

This section was about managing anxiety in the world of work. These were the main ideas.

1. **Understand that your work is a relationship system.** Like any group of humans, coworkers are constantly reacting to one another. The ability to zoom out and recognize those anxiety-managing strategies can keep you from blaming yourself, your boss, or anyone else.

2. **Recognize your automatic functioning at work.** You can't interrupt your anxiety at work until you've spent a good amount of time observing how you function. Perhaps you overfunction for colleagues who are less capable, or maybe you distance yourself from difficult people.

3. **Self-regulate by managing your emotions and thinking for yourself.** In our attempts to keep things calm, we often try to make others change their behaviors. A more differentiated person can stay focused on being responsible for themselves. They practice managing their anxiety and clarifying their thinking before they communicate with others.

4. **Be willing to sit with temporary anxiety to achieve long-term calmness.** Interrupting your automatic functioning requires tolerating a certain amount of discomfort. More differentiated people can recognize that some anxiety is unavoidable when they live out their principles.

5. **Stay focused on your best thinking and not winning approval.** All humans crave approval and praise, especially in their careers. Less anxious people are inspired by their curiosity and not the desire to impress their boss or their staff. They stand firm in their beliefs when they face resistance, but they are also flexible enough to be open to other people's thinking.

Part Four

✳ ✳ ✳

YOUR ANXIOUS WORLD

CHAPTER 16

Smart Phones and Social Media

As we distribute ourselves, we may abandon ourselves.

—*Sherry Turkle,* Alone Together

Clare was living her best life. Or at least that was the story her social media accounts told. It was the spring semester of her senior year of college. Her Instagram featured an international affairs major ready to take on the world. She had thousands of Twitter followers who devoured her opinions on global events. Facebook friends from back home were dazzled by her exciting life in the big city. And her constant Snaps broadcast a senior year full of tasteful partying and solid friendships.

But behind the scenes, the clock was ticking. Post-graduation plans, or lack thereof, had left everyone on edge, including Clare. Her roommates resumed arguments about cleaning responsibilities they'd resolved two years ago. Her parents were wondering if they'd shelled out all that tuition money for nothing. A new guy she liked was impossible to read. All these worries and a failed midterm had given Clare one fat panic attack.

When Clare came to therapy, I noticed that she had her phone in a death grip. She was waiting to hear back from her professor to see if she could do anything to boost her grade. Her mother was calling to see if she was okay. Her roommates were lighting up WhatsApp with their toilet cleaning parley. Her phone broadcast everyone else's thoughts but made it difficult for Clare to find her own.

It's funny how such a tiny box can be such a convenience and a nightmare. A smart phone's computing power is millions of times more powerful than the ones that got us to the moon. But its most troublesome feature is its ability to transmit our anxiety to others at any given moment. Psychologists are racing to define our maladaptive relationships with our phones, so that they can give people a diagnosis. They coin phrases like "smart phone addiction" or "problematic Internet use" to define our dependence on our screens. But what if our screen dependence is simply a symptom of a much larger process? What do we miss when we put our focus on the technology and not where it should be—on ourselves?

Recognize Your Autopilot

We all love to blame our phones for ushering in this increasingly anxious era. And why not? You certainly seem more anxious than that grandpa with the duct-taped flip phone. But I bet you've been paying attention, and you remember that we miss the big picture when we lapse into cause-and-effect thinking. We end up focused on the symptoms, instead of the systems that birth them.

Your phone is an innocent bystander amid real relationship tensions. It merely makes it easier for us to do what we've already been doing since the dawn of time, which is trying our best to calm things down. Think about it: Five hundred years ago, if you wanted to distance yourself from people, you had to pack up and leave your village. If you wanted to complain about your spouse at three a.m., you had to go and wake the neighbors. Now we have delivery apps to shield us from human interaction. We have group chats so we can complain to our friends on a transatlantic flight. Technology makes it easier for us to do what we were already going to do. It makes our automatic behaviors that much more automatic.

To get a better sense of her autopilot, I asked Clare to tell me how she used her phone when she felt distressed. Emergency responder #1 was usually her mother, whom she texted as soon as she felt uneasy about academics or her future. If one particular roommate was disturbing the peace, she usually messaged the others to have them join her fury. Clare also realized that when she felt jealous of friends who had post-graduation plans nailed down, she tended to avoid replying to their messages. Here were concrete examples of underfunctioning, triangles, and distance—all automatic, anxiety-managing strategies that Clare could employ via her phone.

Clare didn't need to throw her phone in a dumpster just yet—it could be useful because it gave her a record of her behaviors. She didn't have to rely on her memory to guess how she acted when she was anxious—she simply could look at her communication history.

Your phone is a treasure trove of anxiety data. And since observing is the first step in calming down, looking at your phone history is a great way to start calming down. These days, the call to know thyself is more like, "Know thy texting habits." Because the data doesn't lie! If you're not sure what to look for, let me give you a list of anxious phone behaviors. Have you ever done any of these things?

Have you ever:
- ignored a message that made you reactive?
- made fun of someone via text?
- begged for reassurance when you felt insecure?
- asked someone a question you could easily Google?
- zoned out of a conversation by checking apps?
- sent an angry message before you could talk to someone?

- lurked on the social media of someone you dislike?
- picked a public fight online?

I feel personally attacked—don't you? This list demonstrates how there are so many opportunities for maturity when we pick up our phones. You don't have to wait for an opportunity to come—there is literally one every time you get a message or feel inclined to send one.

When Clare scrolled through her phone archives, she saw how seemingly random and harmless exchanges were opportunities for her to be a calmer and more thoughtful person. She could try to calm herself down before she asked her mom for reassurance. She could solve problems with individual roommates instead of triangling in the rest of them. She could move toward people she envied and be vulnerable about her own challenges. She suspected that the more she became this mature version of herself, the less she'd sweat about everyday problems.

Social Media and the Pseudo-Self

As Clare kept observing her behaviors, she began to notice how much she was anxiously focused on her social media. She counted every follow on Twitter and every like on Facebook. She knew the name of every friend who'd seen her carefully scripted Instagram stories and never responded to them. She was spending so much energy convincing everyone that she had it together that there was little energy left for her to *actually get it together*. She wanted to persuade everyone, including herself, that she was more successful than she felt. She cared a lot about creating the perception that she didn't care. It was exhausting.

Social media had become another quick route for Clare to calm her anxiety. If Clare felt panicked about her future, she'd post a

Snapchat story reel about an esoteric panel discussion she attended. If she felt like a mess, she'd lurk on the Twitter feed of people she loathed and diagnose their neuroses. If she worried that the new guy didn't really like her, she'd post pictures of herself with other guys on her Instagram feed. And this strategy worked! She felt perfectly competent—for about five whole minutes. Then the high wore off, and she needed to do it all over again.

I've talked a lot about how our pseudo-self can make us appear more or less capable than we really are. Social media is what your pseudo-self eats for breakfast. When you have a constant audience, the temptation to borrow confidence is almost irresistible. Especially when you're anxious. I often tell clients that Facebook "likes" are the Burger King of self-confidence—why cook a delicious, healthy meal after a twelve-hour day when there's a Double Whopper across the street? We know we deserve better, but it's just so damn easy.

Every time you feel like using social media to inflate or deprecate yourself is an opportunity to present a little bit more of your solid self to the world. Let's take a look at what it might look like to flip a pseudo-self habit into a more principled response.

Let's Practice!

Pseudo-Self: Taking thirty-six thousand selfies before you find the right one.
Solid Self: Allowing your friends to post pictures of your regular old self.

Pseudo-Self: Sending your friend a snap from the gym with a self-deprecating joke.
Solid Self: Being honest about your health goals and what it will take to get there.

Pseudo-Self: Lurking on xenophobic Uncle Jim's Facebook feed to feel good about yourself.

Solid Self: Challenging your own prejudices by educating and examining yourself.

Pseudo-Self: Arguing with strangers on Twitter about the latest political news.

Solid Self: Taking time to gather the facts and determine how you'd like to respond as a citizen.

These examples of solid self are merely suggestions. Maybe it is really important to you to get a quality photo for your Instagram because you're promoting your business or you just really value a good hair day. Again, it's not whether a behavior is healthy or unhealthy. It's whether it reflects what's really important to you or whether it's just a quick way to calm down.

Clare could see how her social media habits provided instant but temporary calmness. It was easier to feel smarter than some people on Facebook. She felt beautiful when people blew up her Instagram comments. She believed she had a bright future when she live-tweeted a school event. But by putting herself at the mercy of the Internet, she also left herself vulnerable to feeling dumb, ugly, and doomed if people didn't respond the way she wanted. Or when she stumbled across an Internet person more fabulous than herself.

Clare was tired of the pseudo-self roller coaster of emotions. She wanted a better way to evaluate herself than social media feedback. She needed to sit down and define what success looked like to her.

Is Mature Snapchatter an Oxymoron?

Isn't the Internet just one giant swamp of reactivity? What's the point in being mature if it will make everyone fall asleep or unfollow you?

We live in a society that values immediacy and drama, so the most reactive voices are often the ones getting the most elevated. But entertain this question for me. If someone asked you to show them your most mature online self, what would you show them? Probably not your angry tweets to Pizza Hut customer service. Or the group text where you and your friends make snarky comments about Gwyneth Paltrow.

This intense reactivity of the Internet is often why people delete their social media when they feel exhausted or ashamed. The quickest solution is to cut off and never look back. This might work if you're a monk or a ferry boat captain, but for most of us, our careers and relationships require some kind of online presence. And there are some positives to a digital life. Researchers have found that social media use can improve well-being when our interactions build stronger connections with people (instead of silently lurking on the profiles of strangers).

Your online life is an opportunity for maturity. You'll remember from Part 1 of the book that there are two parts to differentiation: managing anxiety while staying connected to others. After all, what good is being calm if you can't do it around other people? So before you delete all of those apps, consider what opportunities for connection you might be giving up.

I encouraged Clare to ask herself what it might look like for her to work on being more connected with people who were important to her without giving into those pseudo-self habits. How could she be in relationships with people while also being responsible for herself? Here are the principles she outlined for herself.

Clare's Principles for Technology
- I will calm myself down before I text someone to do it for me.
- I can ask people how they are doing instead of lurking on their social media.

- I will try to make space to be with my thoughts instead of mindlessly checking apps.
- I will share my thinking without trying to convince rude strangers on the Internet.

As her first step toward differentiation, Clare made an effort to start sending messages to people who made her feel jealous or angry. She needed to move closer in order to dispel her belief that everyone's lives were exactly how they appeared online. So she sent a message congratulating a high school friend who'd gotten into his first choice for medical school. She was surprised when he admitted that he wasn't sure he even wanted to be a doctor. It felt useful to remember that human complexity couldn't be summarized in an Instagram account.

Perhaps you want me to tell you that in our brief time working together, Clare became this astoundingly mature twenty-two-year-old. That she stopped relying on text messages for reassurance and stopped counting likes and followers online. But I doubt it. I'm certainly not that person, and I suspect no one is. But I do believe that getting a taste of real connection leaves a person wanting more. And that becoming just a little bit more responsible for yourself feels really freaking great. As new gadgets emerge and new social media platforms explode onto the scene, we all will face the challenge of being our best technological selves. Here's hoping that we can stay curious and find our own mature corner of the digital landscape.

Your Questions

Observe

- How do I use my cell phone to manage anxiety?
- When do I use social media to alleviate my insecurities?
- When does my anxiety lead to immature functioning online?

Evaluate

- What principles can help me use my smart phone with more maturity?
- How could I present less "pseudo-self" in my social media use?
- What would it look like to start connecting instead of lurking on social media?

Interrupt

- How can I calm down when I'm tempted to use my phone to manage anxiety?
- What's one relationship in my life that could benefit from more thoughtful phone use?
- How can I stay thoughtful and mature when I use social media this month?

Your Practice

Your pants computer is a goldmine of data about your anxiety and how you manage it. Take your phone, and scroll through your texts, posts, and DMs from the past month. What were you saying when you were feeling angry, fearful, or insecure? What relationship systems were you engaging to calm down or feel more confident? Write down some of your observations, and consider how this quick messaging can keep you from being more responsible for yourself. Then jot down some ideas or principles for how you can try to respond to your anxiety before the autopilot kicks in.

CHAPTER 17

Politics and Religion

Global warming? Sorry, sir, that's just scientist talk. The same people who say my grandfather was a monkey. If that's true, why was he killed by a monkey?
—*Kenneth Parcell, 30 Rock*

Christian wasn't sure he was a Christian anymore. Which was rather inconvenient, given his name and his family. Christian was anxious because he'd been invited to his cousin's wedding in South Korea. Everyone in the family was going, including his older brother, Dave, who loved to cause drama. Dave and their parents had been at war for as long as Christian could remember. As a teenager, Dave stopped going to church with them and announced he was an atheist. When they urged him to study economics in college, Dave chose sociology. Christian's immigrant parents were quite patriotic, and Dave enjoyed complaining loudly about the military industrial complex. Every conversation was always a battle.

The 2016 election had escalated the tension in Christian's family. Dave couldn't believe that Christian still talked to their Trump-voting parents, who worried openly about the state of Dave's soul. "Why can't he just be more like Christian?" his mother would wonder out loud. Depending on who was in the room, Christian bounced back and forth between being the sympathetic brother and the compliant son. He agreed with his brother about politics, and he kept his mouth shut when his parents prayed for their prodigal son.

Tricky subjects like politics and religion have generated anxiety for thousands of years. But in the past few years, the tension in many families and other relationship systems has become unbearable. Some people become aggressive, cutting off from anyone who disagrees with them or provoking conflict at every opportunity. But for many, the tension has shone a giant spotlight on the conflicting pseudo-selves they have used to please everyone they love. When the stakes are high, changing the subject seems irresponsible. Pretending to not have an opinion feels as complicit as having a dangerous one. Because societal anxiety demands principled responses, it requires our solid selves and our best thinking. You must be willing to define yourself to the people you love, even when it's uncomfortable.

As the wedding loomed, Christian realized that he couldn't juggle all of his pseudo-selves at the wedding. Dave would expect him to be an ally, laughing at Jesus jokes and joining his side in debates with their father. Christian's parents would want him to steer clear of Dave. He'd need a few beers to get through the wedding, but his parents didn't know that he even drank alcohol. He was going to have to figure out who he really wanted to be, and fast.

Focus on the Process, Not the Content

As the date of the wedding approached, Christian made a mental list of all the conversation topics that he needed to avoid with his relatives. Questions like, "Where are you going to church?" or "When do you think you'll get married?" were landmines he'd have to navigate with caution. He could imagine one of his Korean cousins asking about the 2016 election, only to have his father and Dave explode into an argument.

In every relationship system, certain subjects have a history of causing drama. The memory of this anxiety is enough to stress anyone out, and most often our impulse is to avoid the subject all together. As you learned in Chapter 5, it's not the content of these topics that causes conflict. It's simply our inability to stay mature when we talk about them. Too many emotions are flying around, and we usually revert to our automatic ways of managing them.

The best way to calm this reactivity is to take your focus off of the topic itself and instead begin to observe the emotional process—to float above the room and take the astronaut's view. This might sound boring, but observing how a group of people manage anxiety can be an interesting scavenger hunt. Events like weddings, funerals, and holidays are particularly good opportunities, because you have many people gathered and therefore more anxiety than usual. Here's a list of common ways that people respond to anxious conversations. Have you ever seen any of these behaviors at a family gathering? Have you ever engaged in any of them yourself?

Emotional Scavenger Hunt (5 points each!)
- changing the conversation topic.
- playing devil's advocate to be contrary
- debating to win the argument
- agreeing with someone to keep things calm
- trying to be the peacemaker
- gossiping in the corner of the room
- lecturing everyone on how to be mature
- not showing up at all

All of these behaviors are attempts to manage the reactivity in the room. Engaging in an emotional scavenger hunt isn't about making fun of your family. It's a way to help you not label one individual as the "problem person" and instead recognize that everyone is participating in the anxious dance. This recognition can completely change how you respond to an anxious situation. The emotional process is sort of like a black hole—you know it's there because you can observe its effects. But in order to really see it, you have to be standing a little bit outside of it—otherwise you'll get sucked into the same old behaviors you always deploy.

I encouraged Christian to look for these behaviors in others and in himself when a conversation topic generated anxiety. By creating an emotional scavenger hunt, Christian was preparing himself to not be surprised by his family. He was thinking beyond simply blaming Dave or his parents for causing all the tension. This could give him some space to ask himself, "What is my part in all of this?"

The Waggle Dance

When you begin to think process instead of content in your conversations, it gets easier to notice other people's anxious behavior. It is much more difficult, however, to see your own part in the anxious dance of debate. Perhaps the most useful question you can ever ask yourself is, "What is my part in the dance?" Note that this is different from asking, "What is my fault?" Because everyone contributes to the process, everyone plays a role. Everyone has an anxious response, because no person can 100 percent escape their own reactivity. Yes, even Jesus had to flip over some tables.

Christian had spent so much time focusing on how his brother and his parents could screw up a family gathering that he had never considered that he might play accomplice to the anxious functioning. He'd seen himself as an innocent bystander, but perhaps he was more involved than he realized.

When I asked him about his automatic functioning, Christian explained that his strategy was to agree with someone until the room calmed down. The more he thought about it, the more he realized he'd been doing this since birth. As a child he'd watched the emotional standoff between his parents and Dave, and the smartest strategy was to just go along with whomever was in the room. Unfortunately, this behavior had become so automatic that he had begun to believe the things he'd agreed on in the moment. He wanted to make his parents happy, so he paid attention in Sunday School. He genuinely liked his older brother, so he trusted his opinion about politics and world events. Twenty-five years later, Christian wasn't quite sure what he actually believed.

We are all like Christian in more ways than we realize. How many of your ideas and beliefs have you adopted or abandoned because of relationship pressure? Your religious beliefs, political affiliation, feelings about sex, taste in music, and favorite sports teams have probably all been influenced by your feelings about a relationship. Let me give you some examples:

- Everyone in your family attended an Ivy League college, so you're desperate to get accepted.
- Your mother is super Catholic, so you've always accepted that Mary was totally a virgin.
- Your father hated the Yankees, so screw the Yankees.
- Your best friend thought *Point Break* was a cinematic masterpiece, so you do too.
- Ted Cruz likes Texas queso, so you decided it was disgusting.
- Your moody ex-boyfriend loved Jonathan Franzen, so you believe that he's terribly overrated.

It's natural for our feelings about a relationship to influence our thinking. But one day you may wake up and wonder whether you might have abandoned your love for queso a little too quickly. So how do you figure out what you really think? Simple—be more like a honeybee.

Let me explain. When there's overcrowding in a honeybee hive, some of the honeybees need to go find a new home. So they send out all their bee scouts to check out some potential real estate. When a scout returns from an expedition, she shakes her booty. She dances to communicate the distance and direction of the site. And the more enthusiastic this "waggle dance" is, the more awesome she believes this potential home to be. Because bees are democratic, the bees keep waggle dancing until there is a total consensus on the new hive site. Sounds pretty fair, right? But here's the kicker—a bee doesn't vote on a site just because her best bee friend is shaking her butt. Intrigued by the dance, she goes to visit the location. Because she simply won't take anyone's word for it—she has to see it herself!

Humans, however, are not like bees. We are a little lazier and a little more likely to assume that the people we love have totally got it right. And that the people we despise must be completely wrong. This is exactly how we end up with cable news networks.

Christian thought he was more mature than his older brother, but perhaps not. He had always believed the waggle dances of family members without considering his own thoughts. He was beginning to see that he and Dave were both reacting anxiously to their parents. They were two sides of the same coin in their positions of rebel and apologist. Dr. Bowen wrote that a person who rejects their family's beliefs as a result of tension in the family is no more differentiated than someone who adopts their family's beliefs without examining them. Both positions are driven by anxiety instead of principled thought.

Maybe you're wondering, "What's so wrong about adopting other people's beliefs?" We've all asked friends whether or not a movie was good. Few of us have time to thoroughly research the history of every candidate for the local school board, and you don't have to become a theologian to get something out of being religious. But what is the collective loss in a family when people don't take the time to develop their own thinking? In a community? And dare I say, in a country?

Thinking for one's self in a group is incredibly difficult, especially when anxiety is high. Most of the time you end up simply conforming to relational pressure, cutting off from the group, or investing all of your energy into forcing others to change. But what if you simply took the time to define your beliefs and danced them out, like a smart little bee?

But What If a Conversation Feels Unsafe?

There's one major difference between ourselves and the honeybees. It is not our job to convince everyone in the hive to sign onto our beliefs. A gay teenager does not have to win over a grandparent trying to send them to conversion therapy. A person of color does not have to educate every white person they know about systemic racism. People are in charge of themselves, and they get to decide when and how they want to share their beliefs. They can determine what is their responsibility and what is not. And often, prioritizing your own safety and well-being is a big responsibility.

This is the tricky thing about anxiety—sometimes anxiety is a sign that you should plow forward and put yourself in an uncomfortable situation. But sometimes it isn't. Ultimately this is up to you to decide. People who have well-developed principles about high-emotion subjects have a better chance of determining what's an opportunity to define themselves and what's a situation in which it's best to protect themselves.

This was Christian's challenge. He knew that sometimes his parents could become verbally aggressive when they argued with his brother. They had never threatened or shouted at Christian, but he knew that this could be a possibility if he stopped agreeing with them all the time. We talked about how it was okay for him to get off a call or leave their home if he felt unsafe. Because sometimes defining yourself means communicating what you won't allow and when you'll pack up and leave.

Now that he felt comfortable having an exit plan, Christian was able to sit down and further define some principles for navigating challenging conversations with his family.

Christian's Principles
- I will take time to develop and write down my own beliefs.
- I will share my thinking instead of trying to win an argument.
- I will anticipate that sharing my beliefs may make some people anxious.
- I will leave if I think a situation has become unsafe.
- I will continue to learn about the world around me.

Figure Out What You Believe

Christian kept thinking about the beliefs he'd adopted to keep the family peace. He was realizing that he needed to take some real time to think about what he truly believed. This would be a lifelong process, but he maybe could get a little bit clearer before the wedding.

Unless you're a syndicated radio host or an eighteen-year-old fresh off his first semester of college, you're not certain about everything you believe. You must take the time to get comfortable with this uncertainty. You also must sit down and flesh out what you believe and do not believe. This is what I encouraged Christian to do. Before he could be clearer with others about his thinking, he had to get that clarity for himself.

Christian sat down, and at first he felt overwhelmed with all the questions he had to tackle. Did he really believe in Jesus's resurrection? That Dave was going to an actual hell for being a snarky atheist? That Dave was right, and his parents were evil for voting for

Republicans? He was swimming in some deep theological waters, but eventually some thoughts began popping up to the surface. So he wrote them down. And he kept thinking about them.

Finally, the week of the wedding arrived. Christian had eighteen hours of flight time to get really anxious about his family descending on the same city. But he was ready to think process instead of content and stay focused on his part in all the drama.

How do you think this story ends? Did Christian stand up on a table during the reception, raise his beer, and shout confidently, "You know, I'm starting to think that maybe God didn't create the world in seven literal days!" Reader, he did not.

But Christian did pay attention to how his family operated. He noticed that Dave wasn't as dramatic as his parents portrayed him. He observed his parents' own self-doubt when they avoided talking about the 2016 election with relatives. He even shared his curiosity about Buddhism to a great uncle who was eager to talk about it. And when a young cousin asked him if he'd ever get married in a church, Christian turned to him and told the truth: "I have no idea. But I'm working on figuring it out."

We live in a society that expects us to know what we believe and be certain of it. But developing your beliefs, and defining them to others, is work that never ends. Societal anxiety will always be present. So we might as well get curious about what we think, so we don't burn out or become hopeless. We are all better resources to our communities when we can stay interested and rise above our automatic functioning.

If you take the time to do good thinking before you begin your waggle dance, people are going to notice. They might not agree with you, but your maturity makes them a little bit freer to think for themselves instead of just reacting. It seems like the honeybees have figured this out, but we humans have got some work to do.

Your Questions

Observe

- How do I act anxiously during difficult conversations?
- How do my family members manage anxiety during difficult conversations?
- Have I ever adopted or abandoned a belief because of relationship pressure?

Evaluate

- How has anxiety kept me from further defining my beliefs?
- What might it look like to approach difficult conversations with more maturity?
- How can I refrain from simply accepting the "waggle dances" of others?

Interrupt

- How can I make time to sit down and write out my beliefs?
- What idea or issues require more research and education on my part?
- What are upcoming events at which I can test out sharing my thinking with others?

Your Practice

It's time to sit down and write about what you believe. Take an afternoon or a few lunch breaks, and start to flesh out your thoughts. You can choose a particular topic, like health care, the afterlife, or whether candy corn is gross or delicious. Or you can just freestyle—start every sentence with "I believe," and finish the thought. When you're done, take a look at what you've written. Which of these beliefs were emotional decisions, and which ones have you developed based on your own values and thinking? There's nothing wrong with following the tradition of your family or another institution. Just make sure that it's a thoughtful choice, instead of an anxious reaction.

CHAPTER 18

The Long Game

> You have inherited a lifetime of tribulation. Everybody has inherited it. Take it over, make the most of it, and when you have decided you know the right way, do the best you can with it.
>
> —Murray Bowen

I have always been an anxious person. When I was a kid, let's just say I did not have a reality-based relationship with the world. At bedtime, if my parents didn't say they loved me, then they were definitely going to die. If I jumped into bed from my left foot, then I was definitely going to die. If I left my stuffed tiger on top of the air vent, then he absolutely was going to explode and burn the house down. My little kid brain saw a world that teetered on the brink of spontaneous combustion.

In addition to these imagined threats, I had real experiences that confirmed my instinct to prepare for the worst. I feared that my father's alcoholism would drive my parents apart. When I was nineteen, my mother was diagnosed with cancer, and three weeks later she died from a heart attack. My brain learned that disaster could strike at any moment, so I acted as if this were true. It didn't help that the word "anxiety" wasn't even on my radar.

On the outside, I didn't seem that anxious. I excelled in school, and my pseudo-self gobbled up the praise of my teachers and family. Besides my catastrophizing, I was a happy kid because I could be the best. But then I went to college, and I wasn't the valedictorian anymore. And then my mom died, and I didn't have her approval anymore. Can you guess what happened? My streak of overachieving sputtered and stalled. I became depressed and anxious, questioning my career path, my beliefs, and my abilities.

When you're knee-deep in the rubble of your self-esteem, you have to find new strategies for managing your anxiety. Like most people, I found some pretty terrible ways of calming down. I shopped too much. I dropped out of grad school. I maybe watched *Cheers* too many times. But along the way I got curious about my anxious functioning. I became a therapist because I wanted to understand how people picked up different cards from the ones they had been dealt in life. I wanted to know how people built a more solid sense of self than the one the universe had given them.

I count myself lucky that I became connected to Dr. Bowen's ideas and the brilliant people who kept the theory alive. This isn't easy, because these days people want fewer symptoms as fast as possible. So can you think of anything less sexy than the idea that change is slow and difficult and requires a lot of contact with your family? But I believe it!

I don't pretend to be the most differentiated person in the world, or even in an elevator. But I want to close the book by sharing a little bit about the difference that the ideas in Bowen theory have made in my own life. And to give you space to consider what a lifetime of observing, evaluating, and interrupting your anxious functioning could mean for your own story and the world.

Be Less Responsible for Everyone Else

When my husband and I got married, we wrote our vows together. We made a lot of important promises to each other, like loving each other's families and never showing our children the *Star Wars* prequels. But the most important vow that I made to my husband was that I would take responsibility for myself and let him do the same.

You see, I am a helper. My mother was a helper, and so was her mother, and on you go. Add any amount of stress to this helping attitude, and you've got an overfunctioner who planned her own bachelorette weekend and wouldn't let you fold her laundry if her life depended on it. My anxiety turns me into a friendly but annoying sheepdog. I run circles around people I love, trying my best to make them go where I want them to go. So it's no surprise that I became a therapist. The funny thing about being a therapist, however, is how quickly you learn that you have little influence over people. Because people are in charge of themselves.

The more differentiated a person is, the more responsible they are for themselves. And the less they are for everyone else. When I first started meeting with a Bowen-trained coach, I got really interested about this idea. So interested, in fact, that I immediately went home and started lecturing family members about the concepts. I told people they were triangling too much. I advised my father to stop overfunctioning. Over time, I began to see the grand irony of this response.

Eventually I shut my mouth and started observing how the people in my relationship systems managed anxiety. I watched my sweet grandmother run around putting extra biscuits on everyone's plate, whether they wanted them or not. I saw my friends try to fix each other's relationship problems as quickly as they could. I watched myself spend entire therapy sessions trying to convince people to stop texting an ex, only to have them double down on it.

I am becoming less responsible for others at a glacial pace. But on a good day, I can catch myself before I jump in and set dinner plans for indecisive friends. I can stop myself from finishing my husband's sentence about a work problem. I can even ask a client what they think instead of telling them what to do. But my anxiety is always waiting for me to get distracted, so it can take over.

So entertain the sheepdog in me just a little, okay? When you finish this book, don't worry about teaching it to other people. They'll be fine. You just do you. Because being more responsible for yourself is the best thing you could ever do for someone you love. It will calm down your family or your workplace more than a lifetime of lecturing ever will. And the best way to be more responsible for yourself is to never stop observing. Study yourself like you're the most fascinating research project that has ever existed. Because believe me, you are.

Embrace the Anxiety of Progression

Two weeks after my daughter was born, some medical complications landed me back in the hospital for a few days. Being away from a tiny newborn, whom I was supposed to protect, was agonizing. I was sleep-deprived, worried about my health, and full of postpartum hormones and new mom hypervigilance. So you can take a wild guess at my anxiety level.

The second night I was in the hospital, I couldn't stop crying. The only thing that seemed to calm me down was watching episodes of *The Office* I'd seen a thousand times before. While my phone glowed in the dark room, my anxiety tried to convince me that I'd failed: "You're a therapist. You're literally writing a book about calming down! Why can't you get it together?"

When you're working on yourself, it's so easy to stay focused on the symptoms. But being human, like Dr. Bowen said, means inheriting a lifetime of tribulation. We have so little control over so many events in our lives. Your boss will tell you you're no longer needed. Your favorite TV show will get canceled. People you love will die. And yes, you will feel anxious. Your heart will race, you'll cry, and you might even throw up a little.

You may have noticed that there's not a lot in this book about the symptoms of anxiety. But is the absence of anxiety really proof that someone has changed? And is the presence of anxiety proof that they haven't? Think about it. A woman who's reconnecting with her estranged sister might feel more anxious in that moment than when they weren't speaking. A man who's getting on an airplane for the first time in ten years is going to have a faster heart rate than when he's taking a twenty-three-hour Greyhound trip. How you feel in the moment is a pretty terrible measure for how you're doing. So please, just give yourself a break.

When you start to work on being more responsible for yourself, you are not going to calm down. In fact, you're going to become more anxious. If you've been avoiding your boss, moving toward them is going to be nerve-wracking. If you've been waking your boyfriend up in the morning, letting him set his own damn alarm is going to feel uncomfortable. It takes courage to not do what you would normally do, to turn off the autopilot and ask yourself, "Now how do you fly this thing?" Dr. Bowen had a term for this kind of anxiety: he called it an anxiety of progression.

So please, don't be discouraged if you find that you aren't as cool as a cucumber when you start to work on being more differentiated. On some days it will feel like a trip to the dentist's office or waiting in line at the DMV. But if you're patient, a funny thing will happen when you're willing to tolerate the anxiety of progression. You'll start to realize that a lot of situations are no big deal. That you can survive rejection, disagreement, and disapproval. You'll see that there are fewer villains in your family and at work than you had thought.

And your mind will have more space to focus on what's really important to you.

My trip to the hospital produced anxiety in the moment. But my decision to bring a person into an uncertain world, to love a child I can't protect every minute of every day—well, that is an anxiety of progression. It's the anxiety that comes with being exactly who you're supposed to be. So we might as well offer it a seat.

Playing the Long Game

People will tell you that if you're not reactive in today's world, you're not paying attention. But does the world need more reactivity? Or does it need more people guided by their principles rather than the anxiety of the moment? Working on being a more mature person is not a hobby. It's not a distraction. It is your responsibility as a human on this planet. It's true that you won't see its effects as quickly as raising a million dollars or marching through the streets. But differentiation has always been about the long game. It's about acknowledging that you are a part of a multigenerational history, a story bigger than yourself. It's hoping that a lifetime spent observing and interrupting what's automatic will ripple across relationships and communities.

But can it really be done? After all, those who can truly rewrite their programming are like the Halley's comets of the therapy world. Most people come in, calm down a little, and shoot out the door before they make any drastic alterations. But I want to tell you about one last therapy client who came through my office.

This woman had changed her entire life. She kicked a drug problem. She was building mature relationships. Her career was on the move. She was forging a life that was the complete opposite of her exceedingly chaotic childhood. Her progress had nothing to do with me and everything to do with her.

"Tell me the secret!" I begged. "What have you been doing?"

She thought for a second, and here's what she said: "I think I'm just learning how to calm down."

The uncomplicatedness of her statement made me laugh. Perhaps it is that simple. This woman had used drugs to calm down. She'd used relationships and accomplishments. She triangled, distanced, overfunctioned, and fought her way through life. But over time she learned that she didn't need any of those strategies to survive. And she didn't need any magic cure from me. She only needed the slow and steady work of learning to be a self. She had shut down the autopilot and grabbed the controls. By choosing how she wanted to respond to anxiety, she was choosing her fate. I can only imagine where that might take her.

Bowen Theory Definitions

anxiety—a person's response to a real or imagined threat.

cutting off—when people manage tension in a relationship by eliminating contact; an extreme form of distance.

defining a self—the process of change by which a person learns to think and act for themselves while in contact with significant others.

differentiation—one's ability to be in contact with others while retaining the ability to think for oneself.

distance—when people manage tension in a relationship through reduced contact.

emotional distance—when people manage tension by not sharing their thinking about important subjects; people can be in contact but still be emotionally distant.

emotional process—the relationship patterns that emerge to manage tension in a relationship system; common patterns include distance, triangles, over/underfunctioning, and conflict.

over/underfunctioning—a relationship pattern in which one person assumes more responsibility for the other, and the other assumes less.

pseudo-self—the part of the self that is negotiable when anxiety is present; less differentiated people have higher levels of pseudo-self.

solid self—the part of the self that is non-negotiable in relationships (such as beliefs, principles, and so forth); more differentiated people have higher levels of solid self.

triangle—a three-person relationship system; two people often focus on or pull in a third person to manage the tension between them.

My Guiding Principles

If you don't want your anxiety to run the show, you have to determine how you really want to function in the world. Use the space below to write down some guiding principles for operating in relationships, at work, and in the larger world.

My Principles for Relationships

1. _____
_____

2. _____
_____

3. _____
_____

4. _____
_____

My Principles for Work

1. _____
_____

2. _____
_____

3. _____
_____

4. _____

_____

My Principles for the World

1. _____

_____

2. _____

_____

3. _____

_____

4. _____

_____

Bowen Theory Resources

There are many Bowen-affiliated centers in the United States and around the globe that offer training and coaching. The Bowen Center for the Study of the Family in Washington, DC, was the first and was founded by Dr. Bowen. It's an excellent resource if you're interested in learning more about Bowen theory and managing anxiety in relationships. There are online and in-person training programs, free lectures, and other resources to satisfy your appetite. You can learn more at thebowencenter.org. The center can also connect you to therapists and training programs in your area.

If you'd like to read more about Bowen theory, you can visit my website, kathleensmith.net, to subscribe to my weekly newsletter on anxiety. I'd also recommend any of these books:

Brown, Jenny. *Growing Yourself Up: How to Bring Your Best to All of Life's Relationships*. Wollombi, New South Wales, Australia: Exisle, 2012.

Gilbert, Roberta. *Extraordinary Relationships: A New Way of Thinking About Human Interactions*. Minneapolis: Chronimed, 1992.

Kerr, Michael E. *Bowen Theory's Secrets: Revealing the Hidden Life of Families*. New York: Norton, 2019.

Acknowledgments

This book would not have been possible without the thinking of many people who are much more mature and much less anxious than myself.

I never got the chance to meet Dr. Murray Bowen, but I'm grateful for his ideas and the impact they've had on my life.

Dr. Anne McKnight has been a wonderful coach who never once has tried to function for me.

The faculty and staff at the Bowen Center have accomplished the rare act of creating a community where good thinking can happen and people can take responsibility for themselves.

Jessica Felleman was a patient guide who walked with me as we figured out what this book would become.

Renée Sedliar was an astute editor who jumped right in and saw this book over the finish line. Thank you to the teams at Hachette Books and Foundry Literary + Media for their creative thinking and dedication to the project.

Thank you to Lauren Hummel for believing in the book. Carmen Toussaint and the Rivendell Writers' Colony gave me the perfect setting to start writing. Laurie Schultz Heim watched my daughter, and my husband, Jacob, gave up many weekends. Kathleen Cotter Cauley never fails in her enthusiasm for making Bowen theory accessible to everyone. The staff and members of Capitol Hill United Methodist Church provided a constant example of compassion and maturity in an anxious world. Ann Gault, Jonathan Rollins, and many other editors let me write about Bowen theory. I am also grateful for Bowen thinkers like Dr. Michael Kerr, Dr. Roberta Gilbert, and Dr. Jenny Brown, whose writing has helped me develop my own thinking.

And of course, I'd like to thank my family. You have never failed to be a fascinating playground for learning to be a self.

Index

INDEX